America NEEDS A Time-Out

NATIONAL SECURITY MOM 2

GINA M. BENNETT

Wyatt-MacKenzie Publishing
DEADWOOD, OREGON

"Gina Bennett is one of the leading national security officials in the United States and she also brings additional perspective as the mother of five kids to the question: How can we make the country more secure? Bennett does so in an accessible, thoughtful and interesting way."

PETER BERGEN
Author of *Manhunt: The Ten-Year Search for bin Laden from 9/11 to Abbottabad*

"This is another of Gina Bennett's gifts to America, and a prescription for seeing-itself-more-clearly in both national security and what it means to be 'America.' This work is a call to all national security professionals to see that US power lies as much in its generosity as in its military might, as much in its forbearance as in its capabilities, and as much in its striving to understand and empathize as in its pursuit of strategic interest. Throughout, Gina presents the reader with the necessary truth that we, too, often dismiss the soaring potential, perspective, and leadership of women in the security arena. Readers should take heed of her call for America to 'grow up' into a capable, strong, resilient, balanced, compassionate, studious, well-groomed, and loving adult. Her offering is a roadmap for necessary change if we are to emerge from 'American adolescence' into an adult future that truly ensures our own national security."

LIEUTENANT GENERAL MICHAEL K. NAGATA

"Offers a ray of hope that our divided nation can find common ground. If you share that hope and want to expand your own thinking about security, READ THIS BOOK."

JODY WILLIAMS
Nobel Peace Prize Winner

"Gina Bennett suggests America needs a time-out, and she is right. If we wish to increase and sustain national security, it is imperative we shift our country's focus from constantly preparing for war, to building peace. By elevating the female voice, and acknowledging the experiences women have used to maintain physical safety, we realize that America would truly benefit if we 'fought like a girl' and fully understood the impact of reactionary versus deliberate decision-making in matters of national security. Considering the deep polarization of our nation, this is a timely book offering concrete, effective steps on how to bring back *unity* to our United States of America."

JESSICA BARTH
Writer, Actress, Activist, Producer, and
Champion of Women

America
NEEDS A
Time-Out

DEDICATION

To my daughters, for their extraordinary patience, tenderness, inspiration, and strength they have so generously given me.

To my sons, for being the kind of young men this world needs—confident in their compassion, courageous enough to be vulnerable, and strong enough to give love.

And to the "Bad One." We will never forget you.

America Needs a Time-Out
National Security Mom 2
Gina M. Bennett

ISBN: 978-1-948018-59-3

Library of Congress Control Number: 2019949751

Chalkboard © Ganna Todica | Dreamstime.com
Author photo by David Kennerly, www.kennerly.com

W
Wyatt-MacKenzie Publishing
DEADWOOD, OREGON

Wyatt-MacKenzie Publishing, Inc., Deadwood, OR
www.wyattmackenzie.com (541) 964-3314

Requests for permission or further information should be addressed to:
Wyatt-MacKenzie Publishing, 15115 Highway 36, Deadwood, Oregon 97430

Printed in the United States of America

TABLE OF CONTENTS

FOREWORD

by Jody Williams, Nobel Peace Prize Winner

Gina Bennett and I make a rather odd pair. She is an intelligence analyst for the CIA and I am an activist who received the Nobel Peace Prize. Gina has spent over three decades in work related to the national security of our country. I have spent just shy of four decades trying to mitigate the impact of US military interventions around the world, on conventional disarmament and, since the beginning of this century, on broadening our understanding of security.

Despite our very different worlds, it is the question of how best to tackle the multiple faces of security in today's world that ultimately brings us together. (Plus, Gina Bennett is smart as a whip and has a wicked sense of humor to boot.)

It is likely that the concepts and content of this book are very different from what one would expect from a woman who is a top intelligence analyst. But precisely for this reason, it is a must-read book for anyone interested in moving beyond narrow concepts of what makes us safe and secure in this world.

Gina explores what it will take to make human beings—in this case women and girls—truly secure. She looks at the insecurity posed by the polarization of our country and offers a different framework than the norm for bridging our national divides. She also shares the thinking of some of the young women she has taught about what it takes to make people feel secure in their daily lives.

Perhaps the fact that Gina and I, independently and through our completely different work, have arrived at similar thinking about security offers a ray of hope that our divided nation can find common ground. If you share that hope and want to expand your own thinking about security, READ THIS BOOK.

Jody Williams received the Nobel Peace Prize in 1997 for her work to ban landmines through the International Campaign to Ban Landmines, which shared the Peace Prize with her that year. At that time, she became the 10th woman—and third American woman—in its almost 100-year history to receive the Prize. Since her protests of the Vietnam War, she has been a life-long advocate of freedom, self-determination and human and civil rights. Ms. Williams has a Master's Degree in International Relations from the Johns Hopkins School of Advanced International Studies (Washington, D.C., 1984), a Master's Degree in Teaching Spanish and ESL from the School for International Training (Brattleboro, Vermont, 1976), and a Bachelor of Arts degree from the University of Vermont (Burlington, Vermont, 1972). Her memoir on life as a grassroots activist, *My Name is Jody Williams: A Vermont Girl's Winding Path to the Nobel Peace Prize* was released by the University of California Press in early 2013.

https://www.nobelprize.org/prizes/peace/1997/williams/biographical,
https://nobelwomensinitiative.org/laureate/jody-williams

AUTHOR'S PREFACE

In 2006, I was invited to give a presentation about balancing work and family. With five children and a long career in countering terrorism, the organizers thought I might have creative ideas to share about how to cope with stress. I honestly did not, so instead I offered that what kept me sane was realizing what I do at work in service of national security is the same thing I do at home in fostering the happiness of my family. I used a few examples of the things we teach our children, like clean up after yourselves and always tell the truth, as the same things we should do as a nation to secure our democracy.

After being encouraged to write my presentation up for a broader internal audience, it was suggested that I write it as an article for publication in a magazine, which I did. That became the book published in 2008, *National Security Mom: Why 'Going Soft' Will Make America Strong.*

I am glad I wrote this book because I truly believe that we have a tendency to make obvious things more complicated than they are. National and international security are not that difficult to understand conceptually. When you think about it, everyone should play as much a role in national security as they do in their family's security, because the world is made up of families. People are part of families—regardless the formats—and the same tensions, conflicts, hopes, fears, practical considerations, etc., that are integral to a family are integral to a nation and the international community. The way individuals interact with each other, whether intimately connected or complete strangers, is at the root of societal and nation-state interaction, too.

I have been a terrorism analyst in the Intelligence Community for 30 years now. I am almost done. As I grow close to the age at which I can retire, I look forward to the next chapter of service. I have already begun it in some ways, teaching at Georgetown University and George Washington University, and supporting the establishment of Girl Security[1] as a member of the Board. I see the next chapter in my career as doing all I can to inspire those who will be doing my job very soon, if not already. I look forward to handing this responsibility over to them so I can retire to Key West and live the rest of my life with music, happy people, and sunshine.

But before I go, I have a few tasks I still hope to accomplish as a civil servant.

In the past ten years, my take on governance as "National Security Mom" has become a bit more mainstream. As a citizenry, we are beginning to fatigue of the "war on terror" and we are recognizing, nearly 20 years from 9/11 and ten from Bin Laden's death, that our counterterrorism efforts alone are not making us a stronger nation.

In my first book, I argued that having 100% safety was not the key to national security. As with securing our families, where we must teach our children to be truthful, ignore bullies, choose their friends wisely, clean up, and be respectful, our national security flows from how we behave in this world as a nation and not from the absence of threats to our borders. I also observed that the lessons we teach our children and the truths we know as parents—life is not a fairy tale, actions speak louder than words, and an ounce of prevention is worth a pound of cure—are applicable to how we govern. Because we all know that it is not the doors we lock, but the love we share, that secures our home.

I believe the comparison of parenting to governance and of family security to national security is as relevant today as ever. For this reason, I wanted to extend this analogy to suggest that America needs a time-out. Although a time-out is a punishment for a child, it is also a critical calming period for both parents and children. Children need the forced isolation to calm down before they can reflect on their bad behavior and understand not only what they've done wrong and the implications of it, but also what triggered their missteps. For the parents, it is a few quiet minutes without the emotional clutter of a kicking and screaming child to consider how they might be able to communicate boundaries or rules to their children more clearly in the future. Rather than a punishment, a time-out is an opportunity for growth and improvement.

America needs this opportunity because we have been horribly unkind to each other. We have only ourselves to blame for that. We cannot blame our behaviors on manipulation by adversaries. We need to understand that Americans make America what it is: weak, strong, great, awful. It's up to us and us alone.

Abraham Lincoln warned that one day America would have to choose whether to follow men of ambition who seek to depart from the pathway set by the Founders. But no matter how influential they may be, we have to take ownership of our choice to follow them. We tell our children, "If everybody was jumping off a cliff, would you?" as a warning not to follow the mob or give into peer pressure. Each one of us must heed that advice because we are the individuals who become the mob and who create the peer pressure. Lincoln also warned about giving into the temptation to go along with the crowd:

> Whenever the vicious portion of population shall be permitted to gather in bands of hundreds and thousands, and burn churches, ravage and rob provision-stores, throw printing presses into rivers, shoot editors, and hang and burn obnoxious persons at pleasure, and with impunity; depend on it, this Government cannot last.

No one who excuses violence; no one who engages in hate speech; no one who publicly bullies; no one who inspires anger, hostility, and hatred; no one who blames and shames those who scrutinize the record of their public leadership; no one who destroys the thousands of dedicated individuals who took an oath to "support and defend the Constitution against all enemies, foreign and domestic" because they had the courage to speak truth to power; and no one who changes the balance of power across our Three Branches of Government to further personal ambition can say he did not destroy this government. If these conditions continue, this government cannot last. If "We the People" do nothing, this government will perish from the earth.

VOICES of AMERICAN WOMEN

In addition to my own observations from the past ten years on the erosion of America's national security, I have included between the chapters of this book letters and essays from women in national security of all ages and stages in their careers. Most of them are young women studying for a life of service in security and government, and young girls who have a vision for the America they hope to lead.

They are our posterity. We owe them commitment to being something better, and their letters and essays describe not only the strong America they envision, but also how they wish to contribute to building her.

These wonderful girls and women represent a diversity of views, and their inclusion in this book does not amount to their endorsement or agreement of all of my ideas and opinions. We mutually respect each other, even when we passionately disagree.

INTRODUCTION
The Definition of a Time-Out

The United States Government, through the Center for Disease Control and Prevention website, offers guidance to parents on how to use a time-out. "When children misbehave and parents try to correct them, feelings and emotions can get out of control. A time-out allows the parent and child time to cool down. The steps below can be used for time-out."[2]

Step 1: Check the behavior and give a warning

Step 2: Tell your child why

Step 3: Give your child a time-out

Step 4: End the time-out

Step 5: Praise the next good thing your child does

This constructive advice **from** the government is good advice **for** the government. Because "we the people" are the government of the United States, it is sound guidance for all of us. I am continually amazed that we fail to see the guidance we provide our children as good advice for our nation. We were all children at one point. We were taught to behave well within our family, and with others. Families make up communities; communities make up towns and cities; and these make up our 50 states. Our 50 states make up our nation. So why at the national level do we think this advice no longer applies?

In my first book, I introduced the idea that the rules we use for parenting and the guidance we give our children are the same we should follow in securing America. This book takes the analogy further and highlights how the indispensable parenting tool of a time-out could apply to America.

Step 1:

Check America's Behavior and Give America a Warning

So, let's take the first step to check our behavior and issue America a warning.

America has been allowing her emotions to get the better of her character. We have let fear, frustration, and anger drive our behaviors rather than living the values our founding fathers enshrined in the Constitution—values that emphasized the general welfare and the blessings of liberty. Today's political discourse does not sound like this. It doesn't matter whether you watch liberal or conservative news or whose tweets you follow, you can't miss how intolerant and combative America's discourse has become. America's polarization has reached extremes that most Americans have only read about in history books. While polarization itself is not a bad thing, the way we express our differences and our unwillingness to tolerate views and beliefs that are alternatives to our own is hurting our country.

This is why I propose that America needs a time-out. I hope we embrace it. A time-out for a misbehaving and irrational child is a wondrous thing. It is a chance to change. It is an opportunity to reflect and find the better version of himself or herself, the child they know they should, can, and want to be. It is something to embrace and not rush. It is a chance to be still and quiet, to slow the heartbeat and the adrenaline, and to find the calm within. And when the body temperature cools, the limbs relax, the screams go quiet, and the crying softens, the child in a time-out finds peace. It's that peace that offers hope because it enables a child to reflect calmly on his bad behavior. And only by thinking about it and what triggered him can he hope for a clean slate and a chance to be better.

Chapter 1

Changing the Course of America's Future
(By Checking the History)

America remains a young nation in the history of the world, but it can't claim to be a toddler anymore. We stand as an adolescent at the precipice of our adulthood and the creation of our legacy. It is time to decide what kind of adult in the community of nations we choose to be. Like teenagers who reach this age and regress to toddler tantrums mixed with the deep cynicism of bitter adults, we are confused. Like that adolescent, America is afraid of how hard it is to be the better version of itself. It is afraid of how difficult it will be to solidify that moral character and uphold it at every turn and with every test the future will bring. It is worried that it will not be capable of fulfilling global expectations of it, which is more stressful to adolescent America than the fear of disappointing itself, because adolescents are more afraid of the opinions of others than they are respectful of their own.

So, like this petulant adolescent, America has been demanding to get everything it wants, squandering natural resources and hard-earned alliances as if they were in endless supply or meant nothing. We have been unkind to each other, even cruel and vicious. We have been disrespectful. We have tested boundaries and disregarded rebukes from those who are not "like us." We have been continually guilty of acting as entitled, spoiled children imposing our tantrums on each other and the world. I think that if the founding fathers and mothers of America were watching, they would utter the harshest of words from any parents, "We are profoundly disappointed in you."

Coming from the national security field, I have continually argued that the most effective way to ensure that America endures in a world of constantly evolving threats requires a different approach than the default one. For so long we have seen our security as a lack of external threats to us. Or even more so, we measure our security by the strength of our physical capacity to defend our borders, infrastructure, and people from the external threats we cannot control or constrain.

I don't see security this way. As a mother of five, I have tried as any other parent to keep my children safe from harm, whether sickness, bullying, accidents, or heartaches. But I know they will experience these things, so it is more important that I help them develop the coping skills to survive these dangers and rebuild their confidence and self-worth by ensuring they stick to their character and integrity. Their values as kind and decent people, and their commitment to living those values, are more important than a lack of broken bones or broken hearts. Every family experiences tragedy. Secure families thrive through them or even emerge stronger because of them.

I believe America's national security is the same. We should expect danger and harm. We should expect to be threatened by external enemies and challenges. But none of those things will change the character and integrity of our nation if we don't let them. The security of the United States rests entirely in our commitment to living our American values enshrined in the Constitution. National security is the ability of our form of governance to endure despite threats and even with changes to the contours of our country.

In the ten years since I wrote *National Security Mom: Why Going 'Soft' Will Make America Strong*, so many significant and wholly unexpected events have taken place in America and the world. I penned this poem reflecting the issues we've faced...

Captain Phillips, Toy Story 3,
Obamacare and Despicable Me;
Abbottobad, Arab Spring,
and the Boston Marathon bombing;
Occupy Wall Street and Greek debt,
Sandy Hook we will never forget;
Mandela says farewell,
Facebook goes public to sell;
England gets a new Prince,
Fighting in Ukraine and Crimea commence;
Trayvon Martin and Zimmerman,
Blind Justitia where have you been?
Rise of ISIS and its Caliphate,
Charlie Hebdo, Dylann Roof inflame hate;
Mass shootings and the Zika virus,
Brexit, Trump and North Korea defy us;
Assange, Manafort and Michael Flynn,
Robert Mueller back again;

Las Vegas lives, take a knee,
Stoneman Douglas children should be free;
Weinstein, Nassar, Kavanaugh;
Roy Moore, Cosby, and still you're in awe?
Standing rock, stand your ground,
Puerto Rican deaths abound;
Stephen Hawking, Kids in cages,
walls, and furloughs and Incel rages;
Russian trolls, Taliban wins,
ISIS will come back again;
Ocasio-Cortez, Pelosi, and Omar,
yes we have come so far;
But still there is no ERA,
what more do I have to say?

I've spent over thirty years of my life, my entire career, in national security. Like so many of my dear colleagues and friends, I have missed kids' birthdays, first steps, recitals, and big games. I've been divorced and I have lost love. We never get the moments back that could have changed the course of our personal history.

We also never get the moments back that could have changed the course of America, and our place in the world. So, when I look back at the last decade, I ask myself: Is America more secure today than it was when I entered the national security field in the 1980s? Are we a stronger nation today?

My answer is decidedly, no.

So before America becomes the adult it is destined to be, it needs calm, peace, reflection, and the hope of a clean slate. We can still be a much better version of ourselves than we are right now. Children never think twice about the fact that they are in learning mode. They know it. I think that is part of the reason that they approach every dismissal from a time-out with glee. They still believe in themselves and their ability to learn. I hope America can be enough of a child, rather than a stubborn and prematurely cynical teenager, to approach both its time-out and its release from it as an opportunity to learn with the humility and zeal of a child. When we get to the end of our time-out, it is important for us to recall these words:

> We the People of the United States, in Order to form a more perfect Union, establish Justice, Insure domestic Tranquility, provide for the common defense, promote the general Welfare, and secure the Blessings of Liberty to ourselves and our Posterity, do ordain and establish this Constitution for the United States of America.

This is our united mission statement. To enjoy the rights of American citizenship requires commitment to this mission. Whether we realize it or not, every single American—from baby to great, great, grandparent—is called to serve and potentially sacrifice their life in service of this Constitution. How? By not violating it, by not asking it to be violated, and by never condoning those who do violate it. We do not place expediency, even in service of public safety, over preservation of the Constitution.

America is a government of the people. Every American has the responsibility of guiding our development as a nation. If you play no part in that, you have no right to complain about the nation we become. Because the government and the American people are one and the same, it is our ultimate privilege to decide what we would want our government to do for us. It is also an enormous burden, and where our individual sacrifice is necessary, to refrain from asking our government to do what we may want as an individual that conflicts with what other Americans want as individuals. The government should do no harm to the Constitution, first and foremost. The difficulty is most often in finding the balance between the government's promotion of the general welfare of the American people while also securing the liberty of every citizen when those two pursuits conflict. Or when adhering to the established justice from hundreds of years ago no longer insures the domestic tranquility of what has always been a much more diversely populated nation. And even more enigmatically, when the provision of the common defense has overwhelmed our national resources quite possibly because it is the only part of this mission statement to which all voting age citizens agree to. But what about our posterity? Our children today will inherit the America we leave them—why doesn't their voice count now?

The world may think America is a nation of self-centered and short-sighted individualism. I think America is the most complicated and demanding ideal in the world. We owe it to this ideal to heed the warning that our behavior is not living up to it.

VOICES OF AMERICAN WOMEN

#1

A letter from Fontbonne Academy Seniors

To the U.S. National Security Council,

We are seniors, soon to be graduates of Fontbonne Academy, an all-girls high school in Milton, Massachusetts, sponsored by the Sisters of St. Joseph. This year we had the opportunity to take an interdisciplinary course involving the study of both US History and Social Justice. As our year unfolded, we came to recognize the importance of understanding the historical context of modern issues, especially when it comes to decision-making and social change.

We reflected upon the promise of America set forth in the Declaration of Independence: "Life, Liberty, and the Pursuit of Happiness," and considered: who truly has access to this American Dream, who does not, and why? Because of globalization, we concluded that the American Dream is no longer confined by US borders—it is a global dream, shared by other countries that look to us for hope, for help, and for leadership.

Through our experience with Girl Security, we equally understand that domestically and internationally, the United States as a nation faces complex issues that must be addressed in order to solve problems, build peace, and protect our national security interests. We, who represent the future of our nation, write to you to express our concerns about what we deem must be addressed in order to protect the human dignity of

Americans and all global citizens that share in the promise that America represents.

U.S. Domestic Security and the Role of Schools

Domestically, we see many interrelated concerns, but we choose to focus on Social Capital, Violence, and Safety. We are concerned that our nation has forgotten its responsibility to "promote the general welfare" of its citizens, as defined in the Preamble to the U.S. Constitution. For example, the widening income gap between rich and poor restricts access to varied opportunities for our country's most precious resource: children and young people like ourselves.

A. Access to Quality, Affordable, and Safe Education is a National Security Issue

Education can and should be an important part of our national security strategy. Overall education contributes to the long-term sustainability of our country. The more sustainable we are, the more stable we are, and the more secure we are.

But in real-time, in real-life, schools today are a battleground. While we are privileged to attend a great private school, others are not as lucky. The burden of the battle for affordable, quality education is primarily borne by lower income, minority children, but the vast effects of poverty prevent children from all racial and ethnic backgrounds from accessing education.

Many of the kids who fall behind, remain behind and become statistics characterized by drop-out rates, unemployment, incarceration, and even death. Many of these statistics are the legacy of institutional racism.

Those who make it to graduation find attending college out of reach because of discrimination, rising costs, and the threat of debt.

Affordable, quality education is essential to our national security. Policies that create access to affordable, quality education for everyone in our society promotes equality, productivity, social stability, and security.

B. School Security is a National Security Issue

In addition to educational opportunity, schools are becoming a battleground for our domestic security, our community security. School shootings and the related issue of mental health services is an issue of great concern to our age group whose peers have repeatedly been killed on campuses at EVERY LEVEL of the educational institutions in this country.

The Second Amendment of the U.S. Constitution grants citizens the right to bear arms, but the Preamble to the same constitution calls for "domestic tranquility," "common defense," as well as the "general welfare."

While the lack of access to education contributes to cycles of poverty, social unrest and violence, stigmas and lack of investment in mental health services undermines the ability of those who can attend schools, and their communities, to feel and be secure. School shootings are the most pressing school security threat; but also in schools across America, young people are radicalizing online or committing suicide due to bullying. We must understand that appropriate investment in community and school mental health services would contribute to a more secure society.

We know that these are complex issues; each one of us spent our academic year completing a research project on these concerns and others. However, we believe that our government can develop solutions. We believe this because each of us, as seniors, designed a plan of action to make a difference, too. We must all work together to protect our country and ensure the future of our democracy.

National Security and Foreign Policy

In the realm of national security and foreign policy, our concerns are guided by a common belief that America's relationships with other countries—the good and the bad—are highest priority. Globalization and the degree of interconnectedness we enjoy have diminished the practicality and societal value of isolationism.

A. US Allies

With respect to our allies, it is especially crucial given the nature of terrorism and cyber security that the US maintain strong and collaborative ties with our traditional allies. Our alliances and treaties with these nations are key sources of support in both good and bad times. We have to think always about reciprocity in these relationships, both giving and asking advice and assistance for major decisions. We need to extend the hand to all nations who are willing to work for a just and peaceful world.

B. Countries With Adversarial Interests and Related Threat

With respect to those countries with adversarial interests such as North Korea, Russia, Iran, and China and the threats posed by those countries including nuclear proliferation, terrorism, and cyber attacks, we must dedicate sufficient resources to protecting ourselves and our democracy from these threats through diplomacy, appropriate sanctions, and protective measures that respect the rule of law. US leadership must, however, keep in mind that the end-goals of our national security strategy must be the dual pillars of peace: security and justice.

C. Emerging Threats and the Younger Generation

While some may say our generation takes for granted our security, we say we are an untapped resource. Our generation will bear the responsibility of developing solutions to emerging issues such as net neutrality, AI, and nuclear proliferation. We are a resource to be tapped, to be educated, to be engaged. We are not solely the reactive consumers of data we may appear to be, or even are at times.

We have grown up in the wake of the attacks on 9/11. We were fortunate to go to the 9/11 Memorial in New York this spring because our teachers wanted to help us understand the context of the world in which we now live. While the experience was overwhelming at times, we were all struck by the selflessness of so many who gave their time and even their lives to help.

This was a moment of visible crisis where the country came together.

Today, we are in a time of crisis, too, but it is less visible; it is a crisis of self-interest, special interests, political interests, and global interests that have all lost a sense of common good. We ask our leaders to have the moral courage to transcend these divisions. When decision-making processes protect the inherent worth of all people and resources are used to support our common humanity, all have access to the Life, Liberty, and Pursuit of

Happiness that are the hope and promise that our country can become. This is the America of which we dream.

Respectfully,
Fontbonne Academy Seniors

VOICES OF AMERICAN WOMEN

#2

Essay from a 14-year-old

Don't Make Your Problems Mine To Fix

"Secure the blessings of liberty to ourselves and our posterity"—one of the fundamental rules the Founding Fathers wrote that our country fails to meet. The goal of the Constitution was to lay out a plan for our government and create guidelines to follow, but if these guidelines aren't being met, why do we still use it? If I don't feel safe, is the government to blame? Are we all treated equally or is that just made up? Do I have the power to change the direction our country is headed in? These are the main questions I ask myself when I think of national security.

The US is a seesaw, a balance between safety and rights. Finding this balance, however, is one of the biggest challenges our country faces. If too many rights are given it would be unsafe, but too little and we turn into a dictatorship. I believe we need to re-establish that some rights, such as the right to equality, are not allowed to be taken away just to make us small. Our country has been dirtied by hatred, racism, and overall discrimination towards minorities. I do not understand why the amount of melanin in someone's skin makes people believe they can treat them differently. I do not understand why your religion should affect how people think of you. I do not understand why your gender, sexual orientation, occupation, class, race, religion, heredity, appearance, age or intelligence gives people the idea that they can belittle you and take away your rights just because you are different from them. It shouldn't matter to you or anyone else because everyone is different and *everyone* is a human. I am not a what, I am a who, and I deserve to have my rights protected by the government just as everybody else does.

As a 14-year-old I am often treated like I don't matter as much as others because I'm younger. Just like any other kid, I find this extremely annoying. If every parent could tap into the brain of their child, they would be surprised by what they'd find. Among many other things, they'd find that a lot of us kids are worried and stressed about the future. We're stuck thinking about college, careers, money, and the scariest of all, what our world will look like. Considering how fast the population is growing, climate change, and unanimous carelessness of mankind it seems that the Earth won't be looking too good in a few years time. I believe we, children, deserve a lot more respect than we get. Since we still have decades to live it feels like we are carrying the world and that we are the ones who need to create new, innovative ideas to save the planet. Now that is terrifying! Feeling like you're in charge of the future may sound nice to some, but in reality it is an absolutely horrible thought. I want to be able to live my life fearlessly, so why don't we all pitch in and save the future while we still can.

My voice matters in this world, and so does every single living creature in this universe, including *you*. For hundreds of years "we the people" have fought for what we believe is right, so why stop now? We need to support each other, lift one another up, not drag each other down to feel better about ourselves. We need to stop being egotistical, get off our high horses, and lend an ear to others for a change. Our opinions matter, but at some point you need to come to the realization that unless we can agree or compromise, our posterity is going to have it even worse. Now is the time to reverse our country's downward spiral, to make America listen, and to create a better future for generations to come. Just as John Trusler said, "There's no time like the present."

Step 2:
Tell America Why

A child is always experimenting with her autonomy. She comes into this world a product of other people, and in her infancy still considers herself an extension of her parents. The toddler and pre-school years are her opportunity to experiment with independence, though she will be constantly reminded of the expectation to play by the rules of her parents. So, when her behavior has gone awry of what you know you have taught her, she needs to be told why her behavior is wrong. This happens because during the process of applying your guidance to her actions, she engaged in some independent interpretation. And somewhere your intent was lost in translation, because let's be honest: not all of our rules are easy to understand, nor are parents always consistent.

All this is true for America. It is helpful to remember that the United States was a product of parents. It was not placed on earth without having been birthed. Our founders were not just creating a new nation, they were breaking with an old one. They separated from their parent, the monarch of Great Britain, and engaged in independent interpretation of the rules they had grown up with. Those rules were not always easy to understand or make sense of either. How did a country that ended slavery within its own borders continue to allow and enable it in its colonies? How was young America to

17

interpret equality and freedom with such mixed messages?

Like a child, America has been trying to do what is right, but the rules are not always clear. The rules do not always immediately translate to any given current situation. The rules for America are all embodied in the Constitution. The parents who created those rules are no longer with us, and for two centuries now we have had to interpret them for ourselves. It should not surprise anyone that we do not always get them right. We do not always behave well. Does any child? Does even any adult? As a nation, we are still learning.

Because I have been trained to analyze, I can't stop analyzing everything around me. All day, at work and at home, with friends, and sadly, even on vacation, I connect fragments of information and observations to create a picture. The 9/11 Commission referred to it as connecting dots. Most often, the picture I draw when connecting any set of dots surprises those close to me. When that happens, I think of Hermione Granger from the Harry Potter series, "Actually I'm highly logical which allows me to look past extraneous detail and perceive clearly that which others overlook."

Hermione delivers this line without arrogance. She's not bragging as much as she is merely giving a description of how her brain happens to work. I think most trained analysts would say the same. Logic is our medium. If A equals B and B equals C, there is no other explanation than A also equals C. However inconvenient the fact may be. I have been trained to think logically and communicate it truthfully to the people in positions of power.

The dots from the past ten years, to me, create an unmistakable image of a weakened America under greater existential threat now than in the past 50 years. Why do I see this? My earlier poem highlights some of the events that make up the "dots" I connect. The dots are events that show America turning on itself, events that demonstrate our distrust in each other. There are dots that are hard to interpret. There are blurry dots that are hard to read. And then there are shadows of dots that could have been, or still might be, that if connected would draw a different picture altogether.

In Step Two of America's time-out process, I want to highlight two reasons we need the time and space to reflect on our behavior. I have chosen these two because they impact every American, young and old. In addition to the picture of a beleaguered America that these behaviors create, I also see the hope of a different portrait. Even the slightest changes in how we approach these two issues would create a much stronger America.

Chapter 2

Impostures of Pretended Patriotism

The image that I think best describes one of America's most distressing behaviors starts with Colin Kaepernick and hundreds of NFL players kneeling during the National Anthem. But it's not the men who knelt that I am pointing to as the disturbing behavior. It's the lack of authentic patriotism on the part of those who condemned them.

In his farewell to the public he had served as its first President, George Washington warned the American people "to guard against the impostures of pretended patriotism." These impostures were men of "cunning" who would disguise their personal interests and beliefs as a love of country. He also warned that foreign enemies would likewise pretend to be friends of America. Washington understood that America is much more complex and sophisticated than a friend who is easy to like. America is hard.

The Star-Spangled Banner's first verse ends with a question, not a statement: "Oh, say does that star-spangled banner yet wave, o'er the land of the free and home of the brave?" Are we the land of the free if we do not tolerate free expression in the form of peaceful protest?

Are we the home of the brave if we do not have the courage to suffer the simple discomfort of watching fellow Americans exercise their right to freedom of expression? When so many have given their lives, not just in war but also in peace, to preserve every American's right to free speech and peaceful protest, how insulting to them to pretend patriotism while compelling citizens to abandon their act of protest.

As someone who has traveled to places in the world where daring to even whisper an anti-government sentiment can land you or your family in prison, or expose you to torture, I believe protesting your government is one of the bravest acts

An open letter to the American public published on September 19, 1796

"In offering to you, my country-men, these counsels of an old and affectionate friend, I dare not hope they will make the strong and lasting impression I could wish; that they will control the usual current of the passions, or prevent our nation from running the course which has hitherto marked the destiny of nations. But, if I may even flatter myself that they may be productive of some partial benefit, some occasional good; that they may now and then recur to moderate the fury of party spirit, to warn against the mischiefs of foreign intrigue, to guard against the impostures of pretended patriotism; this hope will be a full recompense for the solicitude for your welfare, by which they have been dictated."

– GEORGE WASHINGTON

imaginable. Treating the mere discomfort of watching fellow citizens protest as if the sight were an actual threat to America is not only cowardice, it is an attack on America's strength. How much courage does it take to look away at something that annoys you? America is much stronger than that.

For 240 years, America's tolerance of civil protest has been a key feature of our shining city on the hill. The evolving nature of our founding body of law has embraced our melting pot culture to include and protect the expanding diversity of our people. The image of Lady Liberty standing tall and proud to shelter the tired, the poor, and "the huddled masses yearning to breathe free" has inspired millions of oppressed people around the world. An observer in some distant country where freedom is only something to dream about would view the anger by some Americans at peaceful protesters as the un-American display.

> We hold these truths to be self-evident, that all men are created equal, that they are endowed by their Creator with certain unalienable Rights, that among these are Life, Liberty, and the pursuit of Happiness.

These are the rights that so many were willing to "mutually pledge to each other our Lives, our Fortunes and our sacred Honor." So why is it that self-declared patriots say they are willing to die for their country, to die to preserve these unalienable rights they refuse to other Americans? Preserving freedom also means safeguarding the freedom of those whose beliefs and behaviors you vehemently oppose. When protesting Americans risk their fortunes and their honor to make known that they are not experiencing the right to life, liberty, and the pursuit of happiness in the way promised to them as fellow citizens, how can we cast them as un-American? Where is our sense of justice for all?

The solid black dot in the picture of a decaying America is this unwillingness to tolerate what we oppose. When Americans believe that the peaceful expression of alternative views is "un-American," we have destroyed freedom. The attacks by al-Qa'ida on 11 September 2001 woke the nation and government to the disproportionate power of terrorist violence. That trauma shaped governmental action and citizen expectations for decades. It still does. Why haven't social justice movements, like the #MeToo movement, Black Lives Matter, native rights, or fair immigration done the same? Why, when so many Americans experience injustice—whether on the right or the left side of our political spectrum—do we fail to embrace the problem as a threat to our national security?

Abraham Lincoln thought justice was the most important national security issue, not only for his time, but for the future of America. He warned against vigilantism and urged those with power to restrain themselves, reminding them that when the tides turn and they were no longer in power, they will wish for the new majority to show restraint to them. To Lincoln, engaging in "street" justice was a violation of the law, a violation of the Constitution, and that was something he warned would lead America down a dangerous path.

> Let every American, every lover of liberty, every well wisher to his posterity, swear by the blood of the Revolution, never to violate in the least particular, the laws of the country; and never to tolerate their violation by others.

Abraham Lincoln predicted today's America 180 years ago. He warned of a day when leaders motivated by personal ambition would depart from the founding fathers and lead America astray, "Distinction will be his paramount object." Lincoln warns that if this future leader could not achieve this distinction by doing good, "nothing left to be done in the way of building it up, he would set boldly to the task of pulling down."

Lincoln cautioned that such leaders could only succeed in "pulling down" America with the complacency of the citizenry. "If destruction be our lot, we must ourselves be its author and finisher. As a nation of freemen, we must live through all time, or die by suicide" are Lincoln's reminder that only "we the people" can save or destroy our nation since we are, as Lincoln said in another famous address, "a government of the people, by the people, and for the people."

When he gave this speech at the age of 28, Lincoln understood the fragility of America. For a democratic republic to thrive, it had to rely on both the dedication of its successive leaders, and of the governed, to its founding principles. The founding principles of America are all found in the Constitution. The idea of America, the very idea of democracy on such a large scale as the United States, requires constant commitment to the Constitution.

Public servants take an oath of loyalty to the Constitution, not to a political party, Administration, or the branches of government for which they work. According to 5 U.S. Code §3331, an individual elected or appointed to an office in the civil service or uniformed services, shall take the following oath:

> I, (first and last name), do solemnly swear (or affirm) that I will support and defend the Constitution of the United States against all enemies, foreign and domestic; that I will bear true faith and allegiance to the same; that I take this obligation freely, without any mental reservation or purpose of evasion; and that I will well and faithfully discharge the duties of the office on which I am about to enter. So help me God.

This is the oath I took 31 years ago. I still have the pocket Constitution I was given the day I raised my right hand and willingly gave my life to serve America. I knew then, as I know now, much more is expected of public servants, and particularly, public leaders. To abide by the Constitution means practicing, in the way our founding fathers intended, steadfast disinterestedness, which is to deny one's personal ambition and interests while in public service. Everything we do must be in service of the Constitution without desire for personal gain. Those dedicated to safeguarding the Constitution and the capacity of the Federal Government to fulfill its duty to "establish justice and ensure domestic tranquility, provide for the common defense, promote the general welfare and secure the blessings of liberty to ourselves and our posterity" are not the nefarious "deep state." We are the guarantors of the government institutions that every American relies upon every hour of their day —though they are oblivious to it. We are servants to the institutions the public has forsaken, even though the American public could not live without those institutions.

Consider some of the basic activities of your day, and ask yourself how dangerous and inconvenient it would all be without the Federal Government. From the moment you wake up to the minute you go to bed, the most basic activities of your day rely on the constant functioning of the Federal Government:

- Straight out of bed, would you prefer to go back to outhouses? Where do you suppose all that waste goes? If it weren't for the Environmental Protection Agency, we would not have a vast system of collection sewers, pumping stations, treatment plants, inspections and regulations of the wastewater from homes, businesses, and industries.

- How about making that pot of coffee, pouring milk on your cereal, or cooking up some eggs? If it weren't for the Department of Energy and the Federal Regulatory Energy Commission, you can forget about the electricity that powers your coffee maker, refrigerator, and microwave. Without the Food and Drug Administration, you would never know how many natural toxins and bacteria or chemicals are in your food and beverages.

- Driving yourself or riding a bus or train to work? That would not be possible without the Departments of Transportation, Energy, and Justice—to name a few. Each ensuring some aspect of your commute is not just possible, but also safe.

- At work, you would probably like to get paid for the job you do. That would not be easy without the Departments of the Treasury, Labor, and Commerce, among others. Imagine every business having their own form of currency? Not to mention, you would probably like safe working environments, and air conditioning in the summer and heat in the winter.

· Stopping at the grocery store on your way home? Not without the Departments of Agriculture, Transportation, and Commerce, among a few others.

· Want to watch TV, do some work on your computer, or talk on your cell when you get back home? Only if the energy is flowing evenly and the Federal Communications Commission is protecting and safeguarding your right to do so.

· Want to go to bed and feel safe from random looting, the destruction of an unforeseen hurricane, or missile strikes from Russia? How fortunate that the Departments of Justice and Homeland Security ensure law enforcement and public safety across the country. And that the Departments of Defense and State, as well as the Intelligence Community, dedicate their people and resources to ensuring your security.

These are just a tiny fraction of the aspects of every American's day that rely in some way on the continuity of government, the *Federal Government*. And yet, distrust in these institutions has never been greater. The unfounded conspiratorial casting of Federal institutions, and their employees, as the "deep state" has poisoned the relationship between honest public servants and the public that benefits from their work. When civil and military servants commit themselves to supporting and defending the Constitution, they do it with the full intent to benefit the people, not themselves nor their bank accounts. This is the disinterestedness at the heart of public service in the United States.

So critical is this practice of disinterested public service that the Founding Fathers warned against allowing merchants and businessmen into public service. They feared their business interests would tempt them from serving the public. Lincoln, too, warned that grave danger for America lurked in future leaders who put their interests first and who cared more about creating a legacy under their own namesake than that of the Constitution and the Founding Fathers. He understood that blind ambition and a lack of dedication to disinterestedness would drive some leaders to depart from America's founding principles purely to profit their self-interests or satisfy their need for adoration. This is why he urged every citizen to remember their responsibility to protect America from being destroyed from within, not just from threats posed by external enemies. Because Lincoln knew that only Americans pose an existential threat to America.

True patriots are brave enough to offer the same respect they demand for themselves to those with whom they vehemently disagree because that is precisely what America's Constitution requires. If we want to be authentic patriots, we must remember that giving respect—however offensive or disgusting it is to you personally to offer—is a lot less painful than giving your life and limbs. And we owe it to those who have sacrificed much, much more than their pride in defense of our Constitution to offer that small discomfort.

VOICES OF AMERICAN WOMEN

#3

*Essay by Kathryn Nutting, Masters Candidate
Security Studies Program, Edmund A. Walsh School of
Foreign Service, Georgetown University*

The Constitution of the United States has served as the foundation of this country since its inception in 1789. This document has persisted throughout time, through both internal and external conflict and has served as an international model of self-determination and democratic transition. And while this document successfully brought an end to the monarchy and ushered in a new era of democracy for America, it is not without its flaws and inherent contradictions. These flaws do not manifest themselves as weaknesses, but instead pose challenges to decision-makers who are tasked with guiding the application of the constitution in an ever-changing domestic and international context.

In his book *How Good People Make Tough Choices*, Rushworth Kidder introduces four paradigms, which constitute clashes of core values that are pervasive throughout human interactions, both with one another and with the world. These four clashes are truth and loyalty, short-term and long-term, justice and mercy, and the individual and community.[5] Given that the constitution is designed to guide interactions between the government and its citizens, it follows that all four tensions are inherent in its writing.

One must look no further than the Preamble to find evidence of all four tensions. Truth versus loyalty can be seen in the establishment of the "union" of the United States of America, which requires a degree of loyalty from all of its citizens. This loyalty inevitably creates a tension throughout time between service to one's country and the existence of truths that may tarnish it. Short-term versus long-term is captured by the phrase, "...to ourselves and our Posterity." This statement requires that the Constitution serve not only the present citizens, but also all those who are to come. With this stipulation, the application of the Constitution in any situation must take into consideration not only the immediate, short-term effects on the nation and its citizens, but also the long-term impact it will have on the nation's future.

There is a clear role for justice in the Preamble, as a stated goal of the Constitution and of the Government is to "establish justice." However, the role of justice's counterpart, mercy, is less clear. Kidder looks at mercy as unconditional love for each individual. This creates no tension as long as there is no conflict between individuals. "The difficulty is that the love of several persons is thrown into confusion once the claims of these persons are in conflict" and it is in the adjudication of these claims where one is faced with choice between justice for one and mercy for another.[6] Might justice for one infringe upon the "blessings of liberty" for another? How does this choice, when made on a larger scale upset "domestic tranquility"? To answer this question we have to look no further than the present day, with the growing power of social justice movements, like Black Lives Matter and the #MeToo Movement. These, and other movements like them, have developed in response to the inherent affordance of mercy to those in positions of power by our justice system. The mercy that has been granted to some has been at the expense of justice for many, and it has profoundly disrupted the domestic tranquility.

While the fourth tension, too, can be found within the Preamble, most notably in the first three words "We the People," it also has a more complicated and pervasive relationship with the document and its creation. The foundation of the United States of America and the writing of the Constitution were built upon the tension between the individual and community. Kidder acknowledges this, writing, "Individualism underlay the entire process by which the American frontier became a nation. But community stood for everything the new nation longed to become."[7] The architects of the Constitution had fought for a nation in which its citizens were endowed with inalienable rights to "Life, Liberty, and the Pursuit of Happiness" (Declaration of Independence). However, they also strove for a union that would provide justice, tranquility, common defense, general welfare, and the blessings of liberty. In order to establish such a union, they and their posterity were required to make individual sacrifices in the name of the communal good.

Though autocracies, or in this case monarchies, did not promote individualism, they in return required less from the individual, whose desires and behaviors could be constrained through fear and force. However, this new nation that our founders imagined would not be afforded the same luxury, and thus would require more from its citizens. Monarchies were held together by patronage, power, and fear, but this democracy would not have these elements to unite it. Instead, it would need to be formed and sustained by the voluntary sacrifice of its citizens in the form of adherence to laws, respect for authority, and most importantly patriotism and dedication to the country.[8] And so while individuals are granted inalienable rights, the willingness of each individual to sacrifice on behalf of their nation is what has allowed the Constitution to persist.

Though in 1789 the founders did not intend for "We the People" to include anyone other than land-owning white males, they designed a document that would continue to evolve at the will of the people. Such a decision subjects the document to a fifth paradigm, known versus unknown.[9] The architects of the constitution could not have known where the country would be more than 200 years later, but they knew that they wanted a lasting government that was by the people, and for the people, and they believed in the will and morality of these people to guide its application over time. Thus, facing immense fear of the unknown, they allowed their faith in democracy and in individuals to guide the foundation of this country. Perhaps the founders stumbled upon something more powerful than the tension between individual and community: their ability to mutually reinforce one another. Kidder quotes Amitai Etzioni, saying, "It is through community that we find reinforcement for our moral inclinations and provide reinforcement to our fellow human beings. Communities speak to us in moral voices. They lay claims on their members. Indeed they are the most important sustaining source of moral voices other than the inner self."[10] The Constitution then acts as the moral foundation for the nation and for the individual, but its application and its evolution will continue to be shaped by the individuals whom it serves and whom act in service of it.

E PLURIBUS UNUM
Out of many, One

VOICES OF AMERICAN WOMEN

#4

Don't Tell Me to Wait My Turn
Essay by Kate Hewitt, Girl Security Board of Advisors

I am a Bomber, born and bred. The town I grew up in, created by the pursuit of nuclear weapons, is home to the Hanford site of the Manhattan Project. Two of my great-grandfathers worked on the Manhattan Project as their contribution to WWII. My high school's mascot is a mushroom cloud and the classroom walls depict B-17 warplanes. Driving through my hometown you'll pass my favorite dinner spot: Atomic Brew Pub; then you'll see Atomic Auto Body followed by Atomic Bowling, and when you head to see the downtown residences—you'll pass through neighborhoods of "alphabet houses" which hold more character now relative to the cookie-cutter government homes that workers of the Hanford project were once assigned. My first job? Interning at a nuclear power facility.

While I was fascinated by nuclear technology, I wasn't exceptionally good at science (let's be honest) but I loved politics and thought I wanted to become an international human rights lawyer. I studied political science and philosophy at Gonzaga University to prepare for the LSAT exam. I chose, however, to forgo law school and join the Peace Corps to make a hands-on difference. After two years volunteering in the Republic of Moldova, I no longer wanted to be a lawyer but felt a strong desire to serve my country through government. To do so more effectively, I decided to pursue a Master's degree in Global Studies with a concentration in Global Politics at

University of North Carolina at Chapel Hill. My research began by looking at the legality of weapons of mass destruction and morphed into understanding the domestic mechanisms that sustain a country's nuclear weapons program. The research that became my thesis eventually led to my receiving a Herbert Scoville Jr. Peace Fellowship and joining The Brookings Institution in Washington, DC.

It was through the Scoville fellowship that I was introduced to a few incredible mentors and through working my ass off (never sleeping and attending every networking event and happy hour that I could think of) that I met an incredible group of women in the nuclear community. This growing handful of support is what has led to my newest opportunity, much of my success and to keeping my sanity.

Reading my upbringing, it really shouldn't come as a surprise that I now work in the nuclear weapons policy space.

But it is, for a couple of reasons.

First, I wasn't taught about national security in high school. I didn't know how national security issues personally affected me, nor that I had a responsibility to care about policy. And I didn't know what nuclear weapons policy was, let alone that there was an entire career field in this domain. I was 24 when I started to piece all this together and even in graduate school—I really had no idea how to break into the national security field. That is not to say that I would have known in high school that this was what I wanted to be when I grew up—but I would have at least appreciated having the option to consider it earlier in my life.

Secondly, while my entry to, and success in, this field

is much to the credit of a few incredible mentors and their unwavering support, that support was, and still is, the exception and not the rule. I have countless stories of individuals who told me to lower my expectations, temper my ambition, and wait my turn. Routinely, I have been told that I am too young, too blonde, too social, too liberal, too hawkish, too alternative, too assertive, too high-strung. You name it, someone said it to me.

My vision for the future of national security is two-fold. It is one in which younger generations are given the tools and information to gain a sense of responsibility and agency over issues of security from the local to the international level. That information should include options and opportunities for classes, degrees and careers that better prepare future generations for entry into this field, regardless of their race, gender, sexual orientation, perspective, etc.

It is also one in which support and mentorship has permeated the field and education system in such a way that no girl (or boy) desiring to make a difference in national security is ever told that they are too much or not enough. We should be cultivating and challenging the next generation in ways that inspire them to give a damn about national security and support them when they do.

I haven't been working in national security for too long but I am still here. I now work with a government agency in the nuclear security field, a national security niche. I am still here because I refuse to quit when things get hard and I have a network now that won't let me quit when I am thinking about doing so. This field is extremely difficult to break into and arguably harder to survive once you do. But if there is one thing my experience has taught me thus far, it's that I have a duty to educate, challenge and mentor the next generation. And to ensure that the next great idea in national security doesn't fade away because we didn't give someone the tools, knowledge or support necessary to change the world.

Chapter 3

The Tongues We Imprison

The Trump Administration in 2018 unveiled its new national counterterrorism strategy. This was the first articulation of a President's blueprint for combating terrorism in seven years and only the fourth since the "war on terror" commenced. It reflects the fact that terrorism remains a salient threat to Americans and US national security. But the strategy also begs the question of why, given that fewer than 200 Americans have been killed by terrorists since September 12, 2001, do we remain so scared by, and fixated on, this threat?

Fear is why. Fear has always been the greatest power terrorists wield. You feel vulnerable because you have no way of knowing if you will be caught up in an attack. You are not in control. You may be able to convince yourself it's not rational to feel that way, but you can't prevent fear from creeping into your consciousness. The remote possibility of being a victim in any terrorist attack thus compels Americans to demand that vast resources be expended to prevent groups like al-Qa'ida and ISIS from conducting an attack inside the United States.

According to US legal codes, terrorism is "premeditated, politically motivated violence against noncombatants." Terrorism has been called many things: irregular or asymmetric warfare, psychological warfare, the weapon of the weak, an insurgent tactic, etc. While academics and specialists in terrorism define it in any number of ways, the common thread is seeing it as a tool toward a political end, often within the context of a greater struggle, such as warfare or a geopolitical, religious, ethnic, or social movement. It is held as violence with a purpose beyond the act itself, beyond murder.

The act of terrorism means more than the immediate death and destruction. The shock of it, and the perpetuation of fear, is the enduring power of terrorism. Terrorism intimidates because without absolute knowledge that all the perpetrators have been stopped, without absolute knowledge that their motivation has not inspired others, the fear continues. Those who were attacked—either directly or indirectly—remain intimidated and feeling powerless to protect themselves.

America survived the Cold War with its pressing threat of mutually assured nuclear destruction only to be shocked and humiliated by a threat very few saw coming. When al-Qa'ida struck on September 11, 2001, the deaths, the horror, the destruction shook the entire nation. And for nearly 20 years, we have continued to pin our national security on a pillar of countering terrorism and preventing such attacks inside our borders.

No one doubted what they saw on 9/11. No one questioned the need to prevent it from happening again, and in many ways, at any cost. The amount the US has paid to fund counterterrorism is calculated to be nearly $180 billion a year for the past 15 years, totaling nearly $3 trillion.[11] And that's only money. Legislation, such as the Patriot Act and the Intelligence Reform Act, codified a new pillar of US security. The Department of Homeland Security, unnecessary even during the Cold War, was created. All for this new, elusive global threat we know as terrorism.

We have not had another 9/11 scale attack in the United States since 2001, so it might be easy to conclude that the price we've paid for that safety is worth it. We all have to be the judge of that. There is the possibility that the attack was an aberration of history and was never likely to be repeated, even without the US doing anything to prevent it. It is hard to know, but we can try to put terrorism into the context of other persistent safety hazards and threats to our lives.

In the United States, the odds of dying in a terrorist attack are 1 in nearly 46,000. An American is more likely to die from heart disease or cancer (1 in 7), an injury of some sort (1 in 21), an accident (1 in 31), or even murder (1 in 249). Americans are far more likely to die walking (1 in 647) than in a terrorist attack.[12] We don't see much in the way of counter-walking strategies.

Is it rational to be afraid of something so unlikely to affect you? The question raises the dilemma of whether we should accept more risk, tolerate more threat, and spend less focus and blood and treasure on preventing something that may not harm as many people as we once believed. What would it take to make us consider terrorism an existential threat? What threshold must be crossed to convince us that we have to maintain this epic battle with those who use violence against innocents as a tactic of their politics?

After watching the "war on terror" for the past two decades, it is difficult to conceive that a terrorist group might be able to conduct a sustained campaign of terror across America without being stopped. Given how swiftly and comprehensively America moved to prevent another 9/11, it is hard to imagine.

But what if a terrorist group could? Imagine thousands of attacks taking place every day in America, prompting nothing out of the ordinary to stop them? What about the victims? Would the justice system be fundamentally designed to disprove their pain and suffering, rather than finding and bringing the terrorists to justice? What if after decades of a sustained terror campaign, 60 million Americans are grievously injured? Wouldn't that qualify as a national emergency? What would the counterterrorism strategy be for that? What would the budget be? Would we spend money and effort hunting down the perpetrators, or would we track down only a few and allow 95% to escape justice?

There is no need to imagine this scenario in America; it already exists. And the people who experience this terror are American citizens.[13] This is the threat that girls and women in this country face on a daily basis, and for the entirety of their lives.

- One in five women in America will be raped during their lifetime. Right now, that means 32,000,000 women alive in this country will be, or have been, raped. Yes, that's 32 million American citizens.

- One in three women will experience sexual violence, increasing the number to over 61 million. And if those figures aren't staggering enough, the Justice Department believes that 65% of rapes and sexual assaults are never reported, which would bring the number closer to 94 million.

- Around the world, 30.3% experience violence at the hands of their spouse or domestic male partner. That number is higher in the US at nearly 40%. That is not simply ten "points" above the global average; it is another 16 million American citizens. That means 65 million Americans experience terror in their own homes where the perpetrators are protected by societal norms about what happens in a home, and a justice sector intentionally designed not to invade the privacy of households.

Ask yourself if America is really in a position to brag about its national security and American way of life. What is brave about protecting assailants and ignoring victims? What good is our two-million-strong military with its massive hardware and technology and its $750 billion annual budget to the millions of girls and women being terrorized in their own homes? What do they care if US borders are breached?

For the people who still remain incredulous as to how all this occurs without women speaking out or saying something "earlier," please consider the following:

- 130 million women in the United States, that's 81% of all American women, report having experienced sexual assault or harassment, the majority of which occurs before they are 17. Girls are left with little choice but to rely on family rather than law enforcement.

- But against that background, 93% of child victims of sexual abuse know their abuser; 80% were a member of their own family. *The Atlantic Monthly* was correct: America has a profound incest problem.[14]

· Only 0.5% of perpetrators of rape against women will be imprisoned. How do we expect girls and women to trust a system that lets 99.5% of assailants go free to exact revenge upon them for making the accusation public? Would we let 995 of every 1,000 al-Qa'ida or ISIS terrorists after attacking Americans in the United States go free?[15]

If as a child you are abused by the very people who are supposed to protect you, why would you ever consider trusting a stranger with your experience? If at the age of six or seven your mother or father does not believe you, how would grow up thinking that someone else would?[16] As strange as this may seem to those fortunate enough to never experience such trauma, not being believed is extremely common. It is every bit as painful as the assault, and for some it is even worse. Imagine being told that you do not exist even though you know you are standing right there.

This is one set of reasons that children and women do not report. There is no one they trust or trust would believe them based on what they have experienced. They are left to protect the only thing that is in their power to protect—the integrity of their mental wellbeing.

And if you think sexual assault only occurs in specific places by discrete sets of people, Justice Department statistics disagree: rape has no racial, ethnic, religious, age, socio-economic, or political boundaries. Half the perpetrators of rape are over 30, and 57% of them are white.[17]

The average age of a police officer is 39; 79% are white, and 86% are males.[18] This is not a condemnation of the law enforcement workforces across America; one of my sons is in law enforcement. But science has repeatedly proven that our brains form biases to help us survive. The strongest biases are those based in fear because fear is the most necessary of survival instincts. It is an unfortunate bias that so many girls will grow up instinctively distrusting a male police officer, and maybe particularly if he is white, with neither the officer nor the female being fully aware of it.

Every woman—and no doubt every man—has experienced the #MeToo Movement differently. There is no way to adequately capture its significance to half the world's population; or its perceived menace to the other half. Like so many girls and women, the momentum of the movement made hiding my own experiences with sexual abuse as a child impossible. The movement ripped at the last shred of fabric that I had wound tightly around that monster I carried inside since my early childhood.

For decades I had been keeping it in and pretending it did not exist. But pretending I was fine and that my family life was normal did not make it so. It had a corrosive effect on me. Whoever I was supposed to become was lost when that experience in my childhood hijacked my innocence, my mental and physical wellbeing, and my future. Moreover, the pretending for decades later that it never happened to keep my family "happy," only ripped even further at my autonomy.

A few years before the Weinstein case propelled the #MeToo Movement into the spotlight, I had been slowly turning inward to face the monster even while I was outwardly still pretending it didn't exist. But when I saw so many girls and women around the world begin to speak out and to speak up, my own pace of shedding the past accelerated.

What hit me the most, though, without a doubt was watching Aly Raisman confront her abuser in court. I was a gymnast growing up, and though I had very little talent, I still could identify with her childhood. I was amazed at her courage and envious that she could confront her abuser in that way. Watching her, I realized I would never get a moment like that. And I knew that I needed to find closure in a different way. I wanted what I saw in her face: that fierce look of justice.

Anyone who has experienced sexual assault, abuse, or harassment will tell you that the absolutely most dehumanizing aspect of it is not being believed. The pain of the attacks, the exploitation, and the degradation are horrific. But to experience those things, and to experience them over and over, and not be believed, is worse than death. I have often thought that if I had been beaten with a baseball bat repeatedly in my bed as a small child, there would have been no doubt that I was abused. Instead, I was told it was my imagination or a bad dream. I was gaslighted as a child to protect the rights of "boys to be boys."

The disbelief in girls and women who have the fortitude to reveal their abuse is the other behavior in America that I believe has been disintegrating our strength as a nation. Girls and women are half the population of this country. Half. We are not a minority of people, and our courage should be respected. Make no mistake, this default to disbelieve half of our citizenry weakens America as a whole. The belief that it is natural for grown men to be sexually attracted to teenage girls is prevalent in this country. The 1980s was an era of "boys will be boys" by getting girls drunk to use them for sex or "getting them off the hook" by forcing them into it. And girls were seen as "asking for it" merely by showing up in the same space where boys would be. What's more shocking is just how much the past ten years has shown that these notions still dominate the halls of power.

Those who think like that may be able to forget their "mishaps" when they were younger or write off their behaviors as "misunderstood," but the girls and women they threaten, harass, and assault are permanently traumatized. Halsey captured the lasting imprint in her poem "A Story Like Mine" at the Women's March in 2018 (Watch: https://tinyurl.com/HalseySpeech2018) when she described victims as those with "prisoner tongues." Your truth remains locked up because no one believes it and because no one wants to deal with the ugliness of it. It makes them too uncomfortable. You have to suffer with knowing your truth, and to resist allowing the disrespect you receive to diminish your self-worth for the rest of your life.

Where is the justice for women when the entire system and society is biased toward disbelief? Where is the justice for women when their assailants are continually left unencumbered by the justice system to repeatedly attack more girls and women? It's not hard to do this math. Only a half percent of men who commit rape are imprisoned and at least 1 in 5 women will be raped. Either 20% of the men in America are rapists or a much smaller percent repeatedly rape a lot of girls and women. If the latter is true, why does our justice system fail so miserably to imprison them and keep them there?

Politics is fundamentally about power: who wields it and who is subjected to it. All political structures exist primarily to sort out those two questions. There are political systems based on culture, religion, ethnicities, ideas, and traditions. But we tend to overlook the most obvious political system dominating the globe because it is not in the form of a nation state. Rather, it is so obvious that it hides in plain sight. The politics of gender. The politics of sex and presumed primacy.

The most common form of power imbalance is that between a man and a woman. And keeping that power imbalance is a politically motivated agenda. Take the concept of maintaining a power imbalance into any other arena. For example, the leadership of ISIS briefly created absolute power for itself in their Caliphate. How? By eliminating internal challenge through controlling the justice sector, making the laws, enforcing the execution of them, and dominating all aspects of industry and societal norms in their favor. ISIS used, and allowed, violence against anyone who challenged their power. Those who watched were struck with fear, unable to resist or argue when abused by the tentacles of the ISIS government.

Now, bring that model back to America. Men have always held overwhelming dominance in the political leadership of the United States, despite making up only half the population. It may surprise many to learn that until the 2018 elections, the Islamic Revolutionary State of Iran had a higher proportion of women in their parliament than the US had in Congress. China still has a higher percentage than the US, and the US only barely surpassed the proportion in Russia last year.

But men in America also dominate the justice sector right up to the Supreme Court. Men hold two-thirds, or more, of the Judgeships on the Supreme Court, at the Federal and State Courts. Men occupy 87% of local and state law enforcement positions. Men occupy 80% of special agent positions at the FBI. There are only nine female Governors out of 50 states and only nine female Attorney Generals. Only two women have been US Attorney Generals out of 85 in US history.

In addition to the facts of the pure math, there is also the history of American law and culture. Women have been relegated all throughout American history to second-class citizenship. This is of crucial importance because all of our rights in this country stem from citizenship. Supreme Court Justice Ruth Bader Ginsburg, whose life has been dedicated to the protection and upholding of the very Constitution that has left her out, remarked, "I would like to be able to take out my pocket Constitution and say that the equal citizenship stature of men and women is a fundamental tenet of our society like free speech." It is not, of course, because the Equal Rights Amendment remains unratified.

And what has happened to women who have sought justice within a sector that is so overwhelmingly dominated by men—and more importantly—has an inherited legacy of misogyny that has created an unconscious bias so strong and so subtle that most men and even women do not recognize it?

If you still believe that justice is blind to gender, consider another challenge from Justice Ginsburg,

> So now the perception is, yes, women are here to stay. And when I'm sometimes asked when will there be enough [women on the supreme court]? And I say when there are nine, people are shocked. But there'd been nine men, and nobody's ever raised a question about that.

We live in a world where the traditional holders of power have been men. Women have been challenging that incrementally for hundreds of years. The #MeToo

Movement shone a spotlight on how insidiously some men wield their legacy power over women, while the rest look away and the justice system, that men put in place, feigns ignorance.

This may be why in countries like the United States, where women are becoming an equal part of the national workforce, intimate partner violence is higher than the global average. It is hard to dismiss the logical conclusion that men find it threatening to share their inherited place of power and influence with women.

When an individual drives his car into a crowd gathered at a public event to advocate for ISIS or white supremacists, he intends to sow fear—not just injury—among a broad audience to assert his power. The attack creates profound, immediate injury as well as permanent trauma. No one doubts the PTSD experienced by those who were direct victims of, or even proximate to, a terrorist attack. It is a life-time struggle to get over that trauma. It creates a constant sense of fear and vulnerability that dictates your behavior even in normal settings.

When a man rapes a woman, he intends to sow fear—not just injury—by asserting his most primal form of power. The attack creates profound, immediate injury as well as permanent trauma. Yet, everyone doubts the PTSD experienced by women who were direct victims of, or know of, a rape or sexual assault. It is a life-time struggle to get over that trauma. And there is a constant sense of fear and vulnerability that dictates your behavior even in normal settings because you cannot escape a world with men in it.

However inconvenient this fact is to our current legal definition of terrorism, rape and sexual assault are just as politically motivated as violence by a terrorist group.

Power is at the heart of both. Men who commit sexual assault of any kind assert what they believe is their natural right to overpower a woman and to use her body. Rape and sexual assault are just as terrifying as being caught in an ISIS bombing. Rape victims are just as innocent as those in a terrorist attack. The trauma is just as permanent; moreover, women cannot escape having to continually face being with men for the rest of their lives.

What person asks to be shot or blown up in a terrorist attack by having decided to attend a concert or fly in an airplane? Because they decided to fly or go to a concert where they share space with a terrorist does not mean they were complicit or consented to being killed. Neither did any woman ask to be raped. Being proximate to, sharing a meal or drink, or being in the same family with a man who will become your assailant is not consent, any more than is sitting next to a man on an airplane who later destroys it. Being there is not the same thing as asking for it.

If nothing is done in the aftermath of a terrorist attack to help the victims, identify the perpetrators, and bring them swiftly to justice before they can attack again, what do we think would be the result? Would we expect the terrorist to stop? History indicates otherwise. Terrorist groups attack over and over again in pursuance of their power, even when brutally crushed by security forces. When a government does nothing to stop a terrorist group operating within its borders, other nations will condemn it for fostering and enabling terrorism.

It's not complicated. When you don't take action against a violent criminal behavior you enable it to continue. This concept is at the essence of good Samaritan laws. The good men of America who would never think of hurting a girl or a woman in any way but who fail to speak up and demand justice for women are part of the problem. When they do not advocate for our equal rights and for equal justice for us, they treat women as less important. You cannot sit by silently and think that the predatory violent behavior of some men is not your problem. That silence is perceived as permission. That silence reinforces the legacy misogynistic belief that it is a "natural right" of men to expect sex from women.

The absence of focus and dedication of even a sliver of the resources annually allocated to countering terrorism toward preventing sexual assault in the United States tells girls and women that their trauma does not count. And like governments that turn a blind eye to terrists organizing within their borders resulting in the enablement of terrorism, so does the US Government enable sexual violence to continue.

The new counterterrorism strategy commendably calls for more terrorism prevention and early detection of the indicators that an individual may be on a path toward ideological radicalization, and subsequently, violence. There is no reason that those recommendations cannot be adapted to preventing sexual assault through education, awareness, and forthright discussion of the indicators of this violence in homes, schools, churches, and neighborhoods. The now familiar public counterterrorism campaign, "If you see something, say something," is as pertinent to sexual predation as it is to terrorism. Yet we have seen Youtube re-enactments of rape victims seeking help from passers-by and being dismissed as "crazed" or "drunk." Would you treat a victim of a terrorist bombing that way?

Tens of millions of Americans have already been

terrorized and 163 million Americans arguably remain under daily threat. When will we fight this horror as if it were ISIS or al-Qa'ida perpetrating it?

Justice will not be served until those who are unaffected are as outraged as those who are.

– BENJAMIN FRANKLIN

VOICES OF AMERICAN WOMEN

#5

November 28, 2017

An Open Letter to the National Security Community:

We, the women of the National Security community, come from all walks of life and all corners of this great nation. Those of us who have worked for the United States have sworn an oath to support and defend the Constitution. Diplomats and civil servants, defense civilians, members of the military, development workers, and the locally employed staff workers and contractors who support them brave challenging, at times life-threatening, conditions. Our commitment leads many of us to spend extended time away from our families and loved ones in war zones and hostile locations in service of our nation.

We, too, are survivors of sexual harassment, assault, and abuse or know others who are. This is not just a problem in Hollywood, Silicon Valley, newsrooms, or Congress. It is everywhere. These abuses are born of imbalances of power and environments that permit such practices, while silencing and shaming their survivors. Indeed, in our field, women comprise only a small fraction of the senior leadership roles.

The pipeline is not the central problem in much of the national security community. Talented women enter most of our agencies in equal numbers as their male counterparts, though this is less true of the armed forces. At the State Department, female foreign service officers enter at equal rates to their male colleagues. Yet, with each subsequent promotion, the numbers of foreign service women decline, especially at senior levels. Women now compose 15% of all active duty military, an historic high; but the women who are already serving in senior ranks are being promoted far less frequently than their peers.

Many women are held back or driven from this field by men who use their power to assault at one end of the spectrum and perpetuate, sometimes unconsciously, environments that silence, demean, belittle, or neglect women at the other. Assault is the progression of the same behaviors that permit us to be denigrated, interrupted, shut out, and shut up. These behaviors incubate a permissive environment where sexual harassment and assault take hold.

And it's time to make it stop.

The institutions to which we belong, or have served, all have sexual harassment policies in place. Yet, these policies are weak, under-enforced, and can favor perpetrators. The existence of policies, even good ones, is not enough.

We, the undersigned, call on the national security community, including the Department of Defense, the Department of State, the U.S. Agency for International Development, the Department of Homeland Security, the intelligence community, armed forces, National Security Council, think tanks, universities, and contractors who support them, to take a comprehensive set of actions to reduce the incidence of sexual harassment and abuse in the workplace. These include:

· Clear leadership from the very top that these behaviors are unacceptable;

· Creating multiple, clear, private channels to report abuse without fear of retribution;

· External, independent mechanisms to collect data on claims and publish them anonymously;

· Mandatory, regular training for all employees;

· Mandatory exit interviews for all women leaving Federal service.

Finally, this community must also address the serious gender imbalances in senior leadership positions because male-dominated teams have been found to be more prone to abuses and more diverse teams are consistently linked to better outcomes. And we want to see leaders and managers across the national security community held accountable for creating, nurturing, and enforcing a workplace culture that respects and includes women as equal peers and colleagues.

We are proud to have served our nation and to have safeguarded its ideals, and we are proud to have worked alongside the talented and dedicated men and women who make up America's national security workforce. Imagine what more we could achieve together if we took steps to ensure women could work free from fear and confident that their gender will not affect their opportunities.

How will you protect, empower, and defend the women who serve our nation?

Sincerely,
Ambassador Gina Abercrombie-Winstanely
See full list of signatories on page 160.

Step 3:
Have America Reflect

Once a child is in time-out and has been told the reasons she is there, the next stage is up to her. She has to take this time to reflect upon her behavior and dig deep inside to realize where she has gone off course. Your child has to own her own bad behavior first before reaching the conclusion that she wants to do better.

America needs some time to reflect, too. Retracing our steps and considering the guidance from the great men and women of our past is something we should do periodically. America's heritage comes from many sources, so there is a rich history for us to revisit. Like the child in time-out, we have to own where we have gone off course. Looking back at other times when we went astray, and examining how we got back on track, is a constructive use of a time-out. Reflecting on times when we were at our best is an effective way to find our compass again, and to give us hope that we can get back on course.

There are volumes upon volumes of books chronicling the history of America. The next few pages barely touch the surface of one or two defining moments. While I cannot explore every possible reflection America could consider during its much needed time-out, I want to start with the deeds of our founders that were part of the birthing story of the United States. These are not the brave deeds that we celebrate on the Fourth of July; they are the ones we deny.

More than ten thousand years ago, nomadic peoples from Asia migrated to the area we now call Alaska via a land bridge that connected the two continents. Scientists and historians believe these were the first human beings to occupy the north and south continents of America. They were the original Americans. By 1492 when Columbus reached the "new world," 10 million Americans were already living in what today is US territory. European colonization and expansion into North America destroyed the first Americans. Historians observe that by 1900, there were fewer than 300,000. That means the population of Native Americans was reduced by 97% by European colonization.

Imagine today people from any other country—China, Iran, Afghanistan, anywhere—destroying 97% of the US population. We would consider that not just a genocide, but extinction.

The United States and today's Americans have many, many things to be proud of. And not one of us can take the blame for a behavior that we had no part in, no matter how egregious. But that does not give us the right to deny it happened, or even more so, to deny that it still has consequences today.

So, if you are not a Native American and not a descendant of a slave, next time you hear or see activists advocating for fairer policies, justice, and equality based on the continuing and long-term consequences of the history imposed upon them, try to rise above your defensiveness and feel empathy instead. They are not blaming you. They are not asking for you to be punished. They are asking you to understand how they feel. They are asking that their challenges and difficulties be understood. They are asking that their disadvantages at birth be acknowledged.

My uncle's mother was a Cherokee, and though I never met her, my uncle shared with me what she taught him about respecting and learning from nature. He had a kind and gentle spirit. I think of him often and imagine how painful it was to grow up under the shadow of such a dark history. The Trail of Tears in 1838 was the result of Presidents Andrew Jackson and Martin Van Buren's forced drive of Native Americans out of their ancestral homes in southeastern America westward to lands that were strange to them. They were forced without warning to depart what had been their country for thousands of years, on foot—some bound in chains—without food, supplies, or help. Moreover, they were prodded by soldiers at bayonet point while white men looted their homes and belongings.

> *We are now about to take our leave and kind farewell to our native land, the country the Great Spirit gave our Fathers, we are on the eve of leaving that country that gave us birth, it is with sorrow we are forced by the white man to quit the scenes of our childhood...we bid farewell to it and all we hold dear.*
>
> — CHARLES HICKS, VICE CHIEF OF THE ANIYUNIWYA

As America sits quietly to reflect upon its past—great and awful—I hope it has the courage to feel what it should. Feeling remorse for what we have done wrong, as much as feeling elation for what we have done right, is the first step toward healing.

Chapter 4

America Already Knows How to Behave
(Compulsion Is the Negation of Freedom)

As mentioned earlier, Lincoln's prescription for preventing our national suicide was to rededicate ourselves to the Constitution. This might be relatively straightforward if it weren't for the fact that today each side of America's polarized landscape believes it is already adhering to the Constitution. The Constitution does not side with either the rights of the individual or the safeguarding of the community. It does not tell us what to do when so many of our values and policies are diametrically opposed. Both sides' agendas are derived from, and protected by, the same Constitution.

Looking to a different era to reflect upon, the Cold War comes to mind. Senator Joseph McCarthy conducted "witch hunts" for American communists that inspired *The Crucible* and made McCarthyism the term for endorsing unsubstantiated allegations to destroy a fellow American. The Red Scare attacked one of the Constitution's most sacred pillars: the First Amendment. The rights conferred in the First Amendment provide the means to ensuring "life, liberty, and the pursuit of happiness." The First Amendment is the foundation of freedom because the right to be yourself through expression and association without fear is the ultimate freedom.

There is a certain irony to McCarthy's influence at a time when the United States embraced the freedoms of the First Amendment as the core weapon for defeating communism. The National Security Council published Paper Number 68, detailing America's strategy to confront the totalitarian ideology of the Soviet Union. Like Lincoln, NSC-68 called on Americans to participate in preserving the United States through commitment to the Constitution's hardest principle of freedom: toleration of what you oppose.

> The fundamental purpose of the United States is laid down in the Preamble to the Constitution: "... to form a more perfect Union, establish justice, insure domestic Tranquility, provide for the common defence, promote the general Welfare, and secure the Blessings of Liberty to ourselves and our Posterity." In essence, the fundamental purpose is to assure the integrity and vitality of our free society, which is founded upon the dignity and worth of the individual.
>
> Three realities emerge as a consequence of this purpose: Our determination to maintain the essential elements of individual freedom, as set forth in the Constitution and Bill of Rights; our determination to create conditions under which our free and democratic system can live and prosper; and our determination to fight if necessary to defend our way of life, for which as in the Declaration of Independence, "with a firm reliance on the protection of Divine Providence,

we mutually pledge to each other our lives, our Fortunes, and our sacred Honor."

From this idea of freedom with responsibility derives the marvelous diversity, the deep tolerance, the lawfulness of the free society. This is the explanation of the strength of free men. It constitutes the integrity and the vitality of a free and democratic system. The free society attempts to create and maintain an environment in which every individual has the opportunity to realize his creative powers. It also explains why the free society tolerates those within it who would use their freedom to destroy it. **For the free society does not fear, it welcomes, diversity. It derives its strength from its hospitality even to antipathetic ideas.** It is a market for free trade in ideas, secure in its faith that free men will take the best wares, and grow to a fuller and better realization of their powers in exercising their choice.

This was grand strategy. Some would say that we have lacked a grand strategy since the dissolution of the bipolar world. In the early 1990s, we were thrust into global uncertainty. Would we benefit from the peace dividend and be the world's only superpower, or would we, without an easily identified global enemy with which to contrast ourselves, lose our fundamental identity and fade into history?

It may be worth examining the assumption that the Cold War is over. Names and alliances have changed somewhat, but much of what NSC 68 described remains the same because it defined the threat to the free society as totalitarianism. The advocates of totalitarianism go by different names, but the threat persists. At the time

NSC 68 was penned, the USSR was the principal agent of totalitarianism. Absolute rule remains a fundamental political construct in the governance of many nations, including Russia where Vladmir Putin has been uncontested in power for 20 years.

I have replaced the "Soviet Union" with "Russia" and "nationalist" with "communist" in the following passage from NSC-68 describing America's enemy:

> The fundamental design of those who control Russia and the international nationalist movement is to retain and solidify their absolute power, first in Russia and second in the areas under its influence. In the minds of Russian leaders, however, achievement of this design requires the dynamic extension of their authority and the ultimate elimination of any effective opposition to their authority.
>
> The design, therefore, calls for the complete subversion or forcible destruction of the machinery of government and structure of society in the countries of the non-Russian nationalist world and their replacement by an apparatus and structure subservient to and controlled from Russia. To that end Russian efforts are now directed toward the domination of the Eurasian land mass. The United States, as the principal center of power in the non-Russian nationalist world and the bulwark of opposition to its expansion, is the principal enemy whose integrity and vitality must be subverted or destroyed by one means or another if Moscow is to achieve its fundamental design.

The policies, internal and external, and the global ambitions of Russia are no different today than they were under the Soviet empire. The ends remain the same—to achieve regional, if not global, dominance. This is not hard to understand when you recognize how strategically vulnerable Russia is, given its lack of natural resources. Furthermore, Russia may not show any interest in arresting climate change, but it is most certainly designing its foreign policies based on its future resource needs as much as its current desire for power. It benefits Russia to see other nations squander their resources.

The way Russia seeks to achieve those ends also remains the same as it did during the Cold War: weaken the democratic "Western" world. We are witnessing the same mix of false military might, with real military might, and deliberate, long-term agitation campaigns intended to sow division within and among democracies. Democracies are particularly vulnerable to misinformation and manipulation because giving the power to govern to the people through free and fair elections places enormous trust in both the knowledge of the voters and the integrity of the candidates.

The only thing that has changed from the Cold War is the means. The Internet has provided a more effective tactical platform than nuclear weapons. Vladmir Putin and others did not take the words of NSC-68 as mere rhetoric, unlike most Americans. The Soviet Union they once served was defeated by democracies' faith in their citizen governance. This is precisely why the people, not our institutions, have been the target of Russia's methodical campaign of undermining American's tolerance of diversity. Putin is using divisiveness to threaten America without ever firing a weapon. And while Russia has no doubt manipulated us, poisoned our discourse, and exacerbated our divisiveness, we are ultimately the authors of our own destruction, as Lincoln said.

Fortunately, that means we—and we alone—can be the architects of our reconstruction. Russia, nor any other "great power competitor," nor any terrorist group can stop what we can do to, and for, ourselves. We—and we alone—make ourselves secure. Just as the description of totalitarianism as the enemy is still relevant today, so is the explanation of America's strength. NSC 68 also proclaimed,

> The idea of freedom is the most contagious idea in history, more contagious than the idea of submission to authority.

We live in a highly polarized America. To safeguard freedom, we have to be willing to tolerate discomfort and frustration, even red-hot anger, when respecting our fellow citizens who think and behave differently from us. Tolerance is emotionally exhausting, but guaranteeing freedom to all of us requires tolerance. NSC-68 still terrifies Putin, Russian nationalists, and all of our detractors because it was right: "compulsion is the negation of freedom."

Free people have the right and ability to do something more powerful than guarantee their personal safety: reject the societal fear that power-hungry political leaders seek to create to keep us divided and weak. The rise in "nationalist" sentiment is not a surprising reaction to the homogenizing forces of rapid globalization. So many populations around the world feel their sense of identity—whether defined by gender, ethnicity, race, religion, history, or political party—threatened by a world that has enabled the migration of beliefs and cultures at instantaneous speed. Micro-identity political activism is contesting traditional power structures, and traditional authorities are resisting what they view as existential attacks on their identity.

This is no longer a world we can divide into state and non-state actors. Nor is it a world where we can neatly wall off threats emanating from abroad from those originating within the United States. Identity power struggles know no borders in the Internet age. The constant flow of information, barrage of evocative images, inflammatory narratives, as well as outright disinformation and lies, mobilize people to hatred and violence.

Lincoln warned that we could go down a path of self-destruction if we become complacent toward violations of the Constitution, because doing so would undermine our political institutions and ultimately destroy our democratic republic. Thus, the real threat to America originates with our lack of trust in each other because we are America's political institutions.

To rededicate ourselves to the Constitution as Lincoln urged, requires setting aside the different interpretations of our founding body of law and instead finding unity in our loyalty to it. Gridlock prevents one side from compelling the other to accept its beliefs, and is an indicator of a functioning democracy in a polarized political landscape. Rather than exposing weakness in our governance, gridlock demonstrates its greatest strength: the refusal to submit to compulsion and totalitarianism precisely when democracy calls on us to sacrifice some of our wants and needs for the sake of unity. NSC-68 stated:

The free society cherishes and protects as fundamental the rights of the minority against the will of a majority, because these rights are the inalienable rights of each and every individual.

We should never tolerate violence, but we should expect to confront the human emotion of hatred. We should never condone incitement to murder, but we should expect hostile arguments. We should never allow the exploitation of the powerless by the powerful, but we must respect our political institutions if we are to demonstrate our faith in government of the people, by the people, and for the people. When we achieve this kind of dedication to freedom, we will be resilient and fearless in the face of any type of threat to America. NSC-68 sums up the responsibility of Americans who say they are willing to defend freedom:

The free society values the individual as an end in himself, **requiring of him only that measure of self-discipline and self-restraint which make the rights of each individual compatible with the rights of every other individual**. The freedom of the individual has as its counterpart, therefore, the negative responsibility of the individual not to exercise his freedom in ways inconsistent with the freedom of other individuals and the positive responsibility to make constructive use of his freedom in the building of a just society.

VOICES OF AMERICAN WOMEN

#6

Essay by Isabella Sławomira Kopij, Intelligence Analyst, Private Sector Security Industry Operations

Minds assigned to the protection of a country must be sharpened and honed to think in terms of risk. As an Intelligence Analyst for a defense contractor, I define national security as the work of actively diminishing the risk of harm to one's homeland, and this definition has impacted my decision to contribute to United States national security through the private sector. A true threat to national security is not the "danger" to our nation, itself—it is whatever prevents us from minimizing that danger. The implication of this definition, however, would mean that the greatest threat to national security comes from within, through a nation's own isolation from its allies, through internal operational division, and through disconnect between government and citizenry.

Periods in which a nation isolates itself from its allies are a threat to national security, because they result in the nation forfeiting a political, economic, and military mechanism for defense in the global arena. Weakened relations with allies and neighbors may occur due to either a growing isolationist philosophy or diplomatic disagreements between leadership. Regardless of circumstance, a nation's own withdrawal from foreign relations results in the government depriving its state of alliances, intelligence, material resources, and other tools of deterrence. In recent years, for example, the United States government has rejected bilateral and multilateral partnership in pursuit of unilateral action. The nation has severely decreased its budget to the Department of State, it has withdrawn from the United Nations Human Rights Council, it has refused to cooperate with its closest allies in the Group of Seven, and its leadership has exchanged verbal and written altercations with its closest neighbors and allies. Government agencies are then left to work with decreased information sharing, a lowered budget for diplomacy, and a public image of the US on poor terms with its allies. Based on the increasingly isolationist policy of the United States, I pursued security through the defense industry rather than in public-sector diplomacy despite my education having been in Foreign Service. My career choice grants me access to more effective tools and methods of crisis management, in order to prevent impact to my nation's defense assets.

When polarization escalates to the degree that government operations are constantly hindered by internal division, the nation's security may be endangered. In such a case, conflicts of interest result in the issue of dissenting guidance, either stovepiping or circumventing leadership, and lack of focus on the greater mission in favor of personal ideology. In recent years, evidence of this internal dissent can be seen in government shutdowns over divisions on budgeting, the high turnover rate among presidential advisors, and House and Senate Judiciary Committees degenerating into heated arguments over partisanship. For national security, arguments over budgeting may cause delays and improper allocation of resources, and polarization may lead to leadership misinterpreting or dismissing valuable intelligence crucial to protecting the nation. For my corporation's security division, I contribute by modifying and implementing security procedures and operations, so that we are able to combat the threats faced by our government clients, despite any personal conflicts of interest.

Finally, national security may be impacted through societal disconnect between a nation's government and its citizenry. This issue often arises from lack of transparency on the part of the government, so that either society may not fully understand how certain government operations are designed to mitigate the risk of danger, or the government lacks the accountability necessary to justify how its practices ensure public safety. In other cases, this disconnect leads to distrust on both ends and opens the potential for external manipulation and the dissemination of misinformation. Currently, this division between government and citizenry is prevalent in American society, through gag orders on agencies preventing information from being shared, and through public trust in the government having collapsed since the 1960s. The people are made into the enemy on one end, while the leadership is villainized on the other, which only ferments extremism and distracts from larger issues. In my efforts to navigate security issues in the defense industry, I control the quality of the information we share to keep intelligence streamlined, consistent, and transparent for our stakeholders.

No enemy or threat can outrival internal weakness. Times of isolation, internal dissent, and societal disconnect heavily impact security sector efforts to lessen the risk of harm to the nation. My choice to serve the United States through private sector crisis management allows me to circumvent these issues. I contribute to my nation's security by analyzing and managing the risk of impact to its personnel and defense systems during emergencies, in the name of defending the homeland.

Chapter 5

America Knows How to be a Good Friend
(When You Realize Your Child Is the Bully)

Almost every parent experiences a moment when they realize their children is the problem. It's awful. When you hear from a teacher or another parent that your child is a bully, your heart sinks. Your instinct is to believe your child's interpretation of events and to protect him or her. Your instinct is to blame others.

This is one of the worst feelings as a parent. It is hard, really quite impossible, to separate yourself from your children. You are part of them biologically, genetically; that's just a fact. But the act of nurturing and loving them makes them a part of you as well. Every parent feels proud when their child accomplishes some great new feat, or even a very little one. You are so invested, so rooted in their growth and development, that when they reach a new milestone, you feel as if you have reached it, too. Without knowing it, you take a little bit of ownership of your children's accomplishments.

I think this also explains why parents feel ashamed of their children's mistakes. They see it as a reflection of them and their choices or behaviors. Parents are afraid of being judged as bad parents when their child makes an error. This is unfortunate because it creates a tendency to become blind to our children's problematic behaviors and choices, thereby reinforcing the problems. I think it also explains why so often when you can identify bullies, you find their parents defending them. But to have flaws comes with humanity. To have lots of flaws that are changing all the time is especially true for childhood. An unflawed child making no mistakes is living an extremely cautious and isolated life and learning very little.

As my own children have grown from toddlers and teens to teens and adults, I tell them frequently that their mistakes are all on them, but I'll take the credit for their accomplishments. They know I am teasing. I have learned as they've grown older something I wish I'd known when they were little. To allow them to own their successes is vitally important to their becoming independent and responsible adults. That feeling of success is so much sweeter when it's the product of your own hard work and courage. Yet, to allow them to feel the full weight of their mistakes and poor judgment may be even more important to enable them to learn from themselves. They will have themselves, not me, for the rest of their lives. So as a parent, you have to offer the potential for a clean slate when your child makes mistakes and owns up to them. That is how they learn and move forward into a better person.

This entire process is equally true for America.

In the Declaration of Independence, the founding fathers stated, "let the facts be submitted to a candid world." They were keenly aware of a world watching the rebellion of the colonists against the British Empire. Our founding fathers knew that everything young America would do would be scrutinized. If America grew into the nation that the framers envisioned, perhaps the world would be inspired and attempt to emulate our democracy. In our toddler years, we still had the firm boundaries and strong influence of our founding fathers and their direct descendants. As we reached the more tumultuous "tweener" years, the conflicting messages from our early parents who spoke of freedom and yet condoned slavery and an exclusionary concept of citizenship resulted in a traumatic and bloody civil war.

Even the conclusion of the civil war and the Reconstruction did not heal all the wounds nor address all the underlying causes, which would come back later to resurface during the Jim Crow era and the Civil Rights Movement. When faced with undeniably threatening external enemies, such as during World Wars I and II and then the Cold War, our tween-age America rallied to follow the guidance of its parents and show the world a united front. As described in the previous chapter, the ideals America projected during the Cold War were inspirational to dozens of nations fighting the oppression and threat of communism. These ideals drew upon the early framers, as well as, Wilson's Fourteen Points and the Marshall Plan, which demonstrated America's leadership in spreading freedom at the close of WWI and II, respectively.

The Cold War was a test of our transition from tweenagers to adolescents. The immediate celebration and pride that came from not having "won" but having inspired so many other nations, was exuberant. Our ideals of transparency and accountability in governance, and of tolerance for diversity and opposition, were the facts that were submitted to a candid world. And they resonated.

But the celebration faded quickly. Without a common enemy, we were quickly lost. Our sense of identity almost immediately began to fracture. Without a unifying factor as one big tribe, we have splintered into many, many tribes. We see only "us and them." America is so much like the large family whose members are constantly bickering, angry, envious, and vengeful with each other unless or until a neighbor threatens them all. And much like an adult who yearns for "simpler times" and blames the complexities of today on current politics, America yearns for a "simpler time" when it could be itself without challenges.

But those feelings of nostalgia are misguided. Adults yearning for simpler times are not accounting for the fact that life is much simpler when you are a child. Adulthood is hard and decidedly complex. Likewise, America may look back and think times were simpler in its past, but were they? In those "simpler" times, Americans killed 1.2 million Americans in the Civil War, 116,000 were killed in WW I, 15 million Americans were jobless and even more were homeless during the Great Depression, nearly half a million Americans were killed in WW II, over 100,000 Americans lost their lives in the Korea and Vietnam wars, and every American felt the fear of Mutually Assured Destruction for decades during the Cold War.

Compared to the hard times and tremendous challenges America has faced both from external enemies and from enemies of its own making, we live in easy times. We should be strong and confident in projecting the best of our ideals. But are we? Or, have we become the bully?

The US Government has an official website as part of its efforts to increase awareness and prevention of bullying. It is designed to protect children, in particular, but offers concrete definitions of bullying and the types of behaviors that are involved.

Bullying is unwanted, aggressive behavior that involves a real or perceived power imbalance. The behavior is repeated, or has the potential to be repeated, over time. Both those who are bullied and those who bully may have serious, lasting problems.

The US Government definition states that for the behavior to be considered bullying, it must be aggressive and include two criteria:

Imbalance of Power: those who bully use their power—such as physical strength, access to embarrassing information, or popularity—to control or harm others. Power imbalances can change over time and in different situations, even if they involve the same people.

Repetition: Bullying behaviors happen more than once or have the potential to happen more than once.

Moreover, the US Government identifies three types of bullying:

Verbal bullying: saying or writing mean things, including teasing, name-calling, inappropriate sexual comments, taunting, or threatening to cause harm.

Social bullying: sometimes referred to as relational bullying, involves hurting someone's reputation or relationships. Social bullying includes leaving someone out on purpose, telling others not to be friends with someone, spreading rumors about someone, embarrassing someone in public.

Physical bullying: hurting a person's body or possessions. Physical bullying includes hitting, kicking, pinching, spitting, tripping, pushing, taking or breaking someone's things, and making mean or rude hand gestures.

Imagine applying the standards of civil behavior that the US Government expects our children to uphold to the US Government itself! Or even more fantastical, imagine expecting US Government leaders to uphold those behaviors. George Washington certainly aspired to civility and lived his life deliberately in disinterested service. If only a leader as quiet and disciplined could be heard today through the mixture of punk, grunge, metal rock, and other noise America listens to now as a teenager.

America's bullying behavior of late has gone as far as to insult its oldest and truest friends: allies in Europe with whom our treaties were so carefully crafted by a coalition of wise leaders courageous enough to believe in peace. Eroding those relationships may come back to profoundly haunt America. There is an old proverb that says, "A lost friendship is an enemy won." If the enemy we win is as deeply against us as the friends we lose were with us, we will face troubling times. Our European alliances were forged in mutually sacrificed blood and treasure. These were strong bonds. These were bonds solidified, not by sharing genetic history, but by a mutually deep faith in democracy and in the righteousness of governments of, by, and for the peoples.

Of our European allies and in 25 countries surveyed, 70% lack confidence that our leadership will do the right thing in world affairs, according to Pew polling. A median of only 50% have a favorable view of the United States writ large, unlike the far more favorable views of America during the Cold War.

In addition to the injury to old alliances that the US has inflicted of late, there is another factor contributing to our loss of friends, and it is one that merits focus. Among our European allies, 57% believe the US Government does not respect the personal freedoms of its own people.[19] This is shocking when you juxtapose that perception with the eloquent defense of individual freedoms projected by the United States in its grand strategy of NSC-68 during the Cold War.

Confucius said, "Respect yourself and others will respect you." And this is the heart of it. Do Americans respect their own freedoms? If we don't, why would the watching world bother to respect us?

Polling by the University of Pennsylvania found that not even half of Americans surveyed believe that freedom of speech is a right guaranteed by the First Amendment. Nearly 40% could not name a single right bestowed upon Americans in the First Amendment of the Constitution. These are the rights that millions of American men and women have sacrificed their lives to secure since 1776. These are the rights that hundreds of millions of people around the world have been inspired by.[20]

> *Congress shall make no law respecting an establishment of religion, or prohibiting the free exercise thereof; or abridging the freedom of speech, or of the press; or the right of the people peaceably to assemble, and to petition the Government for a redress of grievances.*

Despite the clear language and intention of the First Amendment, almost 40% of Americans support allowing Congress to stop the news media from reporting on any issue of national security without government approval. Censorship by the government, especially when all three branches are dominated by the same political party that can determine unilaterally and in secrecy what should be censored, is a slippery slope toward tyranny.

Today, the rise of self-styled nationalism in America is entrenching already deep-seated, and ill-informed perceptions about America, Americans, and equality. The demographics may be factual, and they point to the emergence of a white minority in America in the next few decades, but demographics are not the point. I would challenge anyone who believes he or she is "white American," to have their DNA tested. All those stories about generations of family coming from "white" Europe will be turned upside down. What's even more fascinating is how arbitrary the timeline for when one considers himself of "European" descent, considering Europeans themselves came from Asia. And for those who believe in the Biblical concept of creation, didn't we all come from one set of parents? What's more, wasn't the division of people into different races, ethnicities, and languages a punishment from God for the arrogance of man in building the tower of Babel? Wouldn't it seem that we should then be striving to be one, humble family again?

Whatever one thinks about race in America, it is entirely beside the point. America was founded on an idea. That idea was the purpose for a Revolution and a Declaration of Independence. That idea was codified in the law of the land, the U.S. Constitution. America is an idea, not a race, not a gender, not a language, and not a political party. The idea of America is the mutual responsibility, accountability, and sacrifice of the citizens and the government to preserve the rights of every individual to the same freedoms as every other.

Instead, we have divided among ourselves into tribes. We look everywhere for "them" and decide that we are not receiving the same treatment as "them." We look for inequalities to complain about, rather than embrace opportunities to be egalitarian. We see the promise of America's idea as a zero sum resource, rather than a well of infinite sustenance.

Our great American melting pot culture has been lost to a culture of exclusionary beliefs. We do not respect what we do not know, so we disrespect strangers or newcomers to our community who look, sound, or pray differently from us. We do not love what we disrespect, so we dislike or even hate those who we perceive as different from us in even the most insignificant of ways. We will not fight for those we do not love, so we refuse— not only to sacrifice our lives for them, but to tolerate the discomfort of allowing them to exercise their freedom of speech, congregation, and protest. If this slippery slope sounds familiar, it should. It may be a basic human survival instinct, but it can be terrifying in the hands of power gone unchallenged. The sentiment, "And I can fight only for something that I love, love only what I respect, and respect only what I at least know," was spoken by Adolf Hitler.

So if we wonder why so many of our former friends and allies treat us with disdain and disrespect, consider our behavior to ourselves. No one respects a bully, least of all a bully who abuses his own family.

VOICES OF AMERICAN WOMEN

#7

Essay by Makayla

In 1883, Emma Lazarus wrote:
>"...Give me your tired, your poor
>Your huddled masses yearning to breathe free,
>The wretched refuse of your teeming shore.
>Send these, the homeless, tempest-tossed to me,
>I lift my lamp beside the golden door!"

I couldn't better capture the spirit of our country than Lazarus' poem "The New Colossus." The liberties that we enjoy as Americans often go unappreciated. I'm not sure when I first realized that I love my country; but I know that I still don't fully understand how lucky I am that I, a "huddled mass yearning to breathe free" can call the United States home. Several moments have contributed to my realization of this gift I've been given, and the subsequent recognition of a duty I have to help defend this country and the values we hold dear.

The first such moment was in high school when I was given the opportunity to attend Iowa Girls State. This program brings high school juniors from across the state to meet and participate in a mock government. We could run for office at all levels—including city, county, or state in the fictitious state of Hawkeye. More importantly, I sat, surrounded by 300 Iowa girls just like me and realized that in many other countries around the world, girls our age, or of any age, could never come together to discuss politics and community leadership. I felt a spark, a moment of appreciation of the privileges of being an American.

Another such moment came shortly after an election that didn't go the way I had hoped it would. I had voted. I had even volunteered for the campaign. I felt that I had participated in every way I could as an engaged voter in our country, and still I was disappointed. I was studying abroad at the time of the election and was scheduled to leave my host country for a trip the day after the election. As I sat at the airport that day, thinking about the elections back home, I clutched my passport. It dawned on me very suddenly that while elections can be won and lost, our freedoms and privileges endure. There I was, walking through the expedited security line in a foreign country just because I was an American. Nothing more than my birth on a particular piece of land had given that privilege to me. Something within me caught flame.

I realized that I had been given a gift and I wanted to help preserve this gift for future Americans, as those before me had given their careers, and sometimes their lives, for me. It wasn't until I got to Georgetown as a freshman that I considered a career in national security. The only freshman seminar left when I signed up was one on civil-military operations. The class was hard and I felt overwhelmed in a room that was dominated by males who had already read extensively on the topic. However, I loved the challenge. I loved that in the national security field there always seemed to be another puzzle that needed to be solved to promote America's interest abroad and secure her families at home. Further, I realized that for every moment I was uncomfortable as one of only a few women in a room debating national security issues, I was contributing to shifting the tide. No tide can shift if people like me didn't stick it out and welcome others to the table.

I'd found how I was going to give back to my country, and I wanted to be part of bringing more women into this critical center of decision-making, the field of national security. I was fortunate to be starting my career after many women had already blazed trails throughout the national security apparatus for me to follow. I'd even been lucky enough to study under some incredible women, like the first female Secretary of State, Madeleine Albright, and the author of this book and CIA counterterrorism veteran, Gina Bennett. I would never have been brave enough to enter the field without their, and others', ground-blazing models. It wasn't just the efforts of women that welcomed me, either. Many of my male colleagues made sure I knew they valued my contributions and made room for me at the table. Nevertheless, work remained to open up the hatches and tear down the barriers to women in the field—and I was excited to be part of this work. In national security, I could grow from a "huddled mass yearning to breathe free" to be a woman "lift(ing) my lamp beside the golden door" to walk beside others who, like me, sought to serve this great country we are lucky to call home.

VOICES OF AMERICAN WOMEN

#8

Essay by Caitlin

My name is Caitlin. I currently serve as an Analyst in Asian Affairs at the Congressional Research Service, Congress's nonpartisan policy "think tank." I am 31 years old.

My career in national security and international affairs began to take shape on August 24, 2008 when I was 21. I arrived in Chengdu, China for a study abroad program on the day of the closing ceremonies of the historic Beijing Olympics. The Games were viewed by the world as China's "coming out party," an indication that China had attained a place among the world's major powers. During my time living in Chengdu, the electric feeling that China had "arrived" was palpable.

Although I was fairly ignorant of global politics at the time, I remember feeling on several occasions that we were on the cusp of a new era in which China would profoundly change the world. This fascination with China's rise and the implications for US interests and the global balance of power fueled my pursuit of a career that would allow me to keep studying this dynamic, confusing, always-surprising country.

I landed an internship with the U.S.-China Economic and Security Review Commission, a bipartisan Congressional commission tasked with tracking the national security implications of China's growing influence in the United States and beyond. A combination of hard work, supportive colleagues, and sheer luck allowed me to advance through several positions within the organization. In my eight years there, I had been an intern, an assistant, an analyst, a research director, a manager, and finally an acting executive director. One of the benefits of cycling through so many different roles was that I learned a lot about my strengths and weaknesses. I found that my love of learning, attention to detail, and inclination to always question my and others' assumptions made me a keen analyst, and I both loved and excelled in this role. Although the pay and the prestige of the management and director positions were exciting and fulfilling, my happiest years at the Commission were spent as an analyst, reading and writing about my favorite topic: China. In fact, I recently took a pay cut to accept an Asian affairs analyst position at another Congressional advisory organization, the Congressional Research Service. I'm not sure what the next step will be, but for now, I couldn't be happier.

For most of my life, the concept of "national security" always felt far-removed. I didn't know anything about the military, terrorism, or war. I thought national security was the purview of generals and admirals and intimidating old men sitting at big desks in the Pentagon. But national security is more than this. Yes, national security is about maintaining militaries and advancing strategies for national defense. But it's also about defending public health against epidemics and biohazards; it's about defending vulnerable young people from radicalization; it's about defending women and girls from trafficking and slavery; it's about defending our environment from destructive climate change and natural disasters; it's about defending cyberspace from thieves, traffickers, terrorists, and adversaries; it's about defending refugees from oppressive authoritarian regimes; it's about preventing the horrors of war. In the end, national security is about people. For me personally, as a China specialist, it's about helping policymakers cultivate a relationship with China that allows the 1.7 billion people living in the United States and China to live in peace even as the two countries increasingly compete in the international arena.

If you were to look at my resume, you might be under the impression that my career has been carefully designed and logically executed in a series of sensible steps. But in reality, the seeds that have given life to my career were planted haphazardly (and usually not by me). Some of the most pivotal moments in determining the path of my career included a snafu over college course credit hours (forcing me to switch my study abroad destination from Malta to China at the last minute), and an erroneous Google search by my dad (who, in trying to look up the website of the Congressional commission on China with which I was seeking an internship, ended up finding an entirely different Congressional commission on China of which I had never heard; I ended up spending eight years at the one my dad stumbled upon). So if you're ever worried that the path of your career seems incoherent or out of your hands, don't worry. In my experience, career paths look tidier looking backward than they do looking forward.

Chapter 6

America Can Be Happy in a Divided Family
(Divorced America Must Learn to Co-parent)

In an October 2004 recorded address, former al-Qaʻida leader Osama Bin Laden lectured the American people about their role in national security. Expressing incredulity at how little Americans seemed to understand that living in a democracy meant the direction of the nation's security was a matter of popular choice, Bin Laden said, "Your security is in your own hands." Letters captured in the raid on Bin Laden's hideout in 2011 indicated that Bin Laden frequently returned to this theme of popular sentiment in America and apparently derived satisfaction in watching Americans polarize over security issues.

Like other foreign observers, al-Qaʻida leaders conclude that America's political polarization is a sign of government weakness and decline. While the Founding Fathers may have trusted that the resulting inefficiencies of their elaborate system of checks and balances would be preferable to a tyranny of the majority, most Americans perceive the political gridlock to be ineffective and embarrassing. Because this self-perception fuels the belief by America's detractors that the nation is in decline, political polarization has become a national security concern.

Americans routinely express a desire to break the gridlock, assuming it is an impediment to governing effectively. But what if it's not? What if there are times when gridlock is the better long-term outcome than the expediency of winner-takes-all? It is hard to see America's bitterly contentious party politics as a positive, but stepping away from it and comparing it to a similar polarized cycle could provide useful insights as well as solutions.

Divorce is a familiar concept to most Americans, and since writing my first book, is something very familiar to me. I remain good friends with my former spouse and he with me. Our children do not lack for love and support and find their parents as unified over their upbringing as ever. So while divorce is absolutely a traumatic process, it can produce healthier relationships than miserable marriages. My children have told me repeatedly how good it is to see their parents happy. We have each shown them that trying as hard as you can does not guarantee success, and that changing as you grow older does not mean abandoning your past. Evolution is not revolution.

A review of literature on divorce describes the many challenges that emerge throughout the phases of the process. A comparable review of literature by noted political scientists, government experts, and historians indicates that polarization in America has involved some surprisingly similar phases. By comparing marital divorce and political polarization, one can transfer lessons learned from relationship experts about surviving a divorce to methods for guiding America through its polarization.

Phase One: The Erosion of Bipartisanship

Many relationship experts consider divorce's first phase as the period preceding the separation when the marital relationship is showing persistent signs of fragility. This stage is often marked by the spouses' diminished abilities to find areas for cooperation. Without regular cooperation, the relationship deteriorates. Leading divorce mediators Diana Mercer and Katie Jane Wennechuk describe this phenomenon as erosion. They note that couples do not usually divorce over incidents. Instead, their relationship dissolves and partners begin to bury the substantive issues of disagreement in accusatory language, frequently sabotaging any chance of compromise.

Mercer and Wennechuk's description mirrors that offered by noted historians and political scientists of the evolutionary process that drove polarization in America rather than a set of specific incidents. Renowned congressional scholar Barbara Sinclair credits the growth of two-party competition in the South in the 1960s and the slow strengthening of the relationship between voters' self-described ideology and their party identification for setting much of today's polarization in motion. On the latter trend, Sinclair points to survey data from the early 1970s to late 1990s that indicated the correlation grew stronger between where respondents placed themselves on the conservative-to-liberal spectrum and the party with which they identified. As the ideologies of the parties grew more bifurcated, Americans apparently grew closer to one party or the other, eroding the middle ground.

Noted political scientist and Emory professor Alan Abramowitz describes the loss of the middle ground as the process of the "disappearing center." He echoes Sinclair's arguments that the two parties offer voters today more internally consistent ideologies and agendas that are clearly quite different from each other. Abramowitz further concludes that voter behaviors, particularly growing turnout at elections, demonstrate that Americans appreciate the choice despite their complaints about polarization. He notes, however, that the most active party supporters represent the more extreme poles, creating the tendency to overlook the moderates.

Other visible trends of the erosion phase include a substantial decline in social and official interaction across party lines among members of Congress, in part because they no longer live in the capital. A similar decline has taken place between Presidents and members of the opposite party. Changes in campaign processes and finance regulations since the 1970s engendered the need for Presidents to focus on their party bases in ever-lengthening election cycles. Furthermore, the proliferation of media outlets, Political Action Committees (PACs), and think tanks that identify with one party over the other has intensified the political debate.

As a marriage unravels, conflicts occur frequently and become evident in the way couples communicate. Criticism, defensiveness, contempt, and stonewalling become the default form of communication between hostile parties. Leading relationship psychologist Dr. John Gottman describes these behaviors as the "four horsemen of the Apocalypse." In a twenty-year study involving more than 2,000 couples, Dr. Gottman observed that he could use these patterns in marriage to predict with 94% accuracy which couples would divorce.

These patterns of conduct also capture today's state of play between Democratic and Republican party activists. With the "four horsemen of the Apocalypse" becoming the default mechanisms for interaction between the political parties, divorce may be virtually unavoidable. Divorce in the political context should be viewed metaphorically, of course. A divorced America may not live in two separate "houses," but the two sides are unlikely to meet in the middle on major issues driving America's busy political agenda. The separation is not geographic, but neither is it esoteric or fleeting. America's divide is driving emotional turmoil and creating battles over major decisions, and most Americans recognize it. Furthermore, polarization has changed the way political actors interact, much like how a legal divorce creates new roles and relationships from former spouses.

Phase Two: Divided Politics Create New Roles and Emotional Upheaval

Divorce's second phase can be the most traumatic because the need to divide the family physically becomes unavoidable. Divorce creates tremendous emotional and practical upheaval as a family struggles through the painful process of separating into two homes. On the practical side, a family's physical splitting overturns previous family roles, responsibilities, and implicit rules. This physical dislocation then spawns new emotional stress.

While married, parents create implicit, if not explicit, rules about who is responsible for which tasks within the family. Around these roles and responsibilities, an individual's identity within the marriage often emerges.

A wife may be the school and social organizer for the children and family. A husband may be budget planner and sports coordinator. Unstated boundaries emerge; children instinctively know which parent to ask for what. All these familiar roles are overturned with divorce, however. Ex-spouses suddenly need to learn each other's roles and the confusion is clear with the first day of separation.

In the political context, the polarizing trends of the first phase have changed the roles of political actors and the traditional balance of power among the three branches of government. These new roles are bound to cause great confusion, particularly as a vast number of Americans are uncertain even about the old roles, according to surveys conducted by the National Constitution Center which indicate 41% of respondents did not know the very basic fact that there are three branches of government. Against this backdrop of limited foundational knowledge, Americans likely will struggle to grasp how polarization has reoriented government interaction.

Beginning with the Executive Branch, trends in the first phase of bipartisan erosion have produced a powerful Executive whose growing demands as a party leader may distract his focus from serving the nation. In his research of Presidential behavior over time, US Naval Academy political science professor Brendan J. Doherty discovered steady increases in the amount of time a President spends campaigning for re-election. Polarization, and particularly the tremendous activist energy at the poles, has led Presidents to focus their campaigning on appeasing their own bases rather than on persuading the significant number of moderates and fence-sitters. Doherty further notes that the way states vote may sway a President's behavior toward it. Former President George W. Bush never visited Vermont, a small state that voted against him. Likewise, former President Clinton only visited Nebraska once. Doherty observes that such behaviors undercut the perception of the President as a national leader.

Another change affecting the Executive Branch is a shift in its balance of power with the Legislative Branch over national security. Law experts have questioned sweeping Presidential Executive Orders designed to deal with terrorism after the attacks in September 2001, but admit that Executive power in the national security realm had been growing steadily for decades. New York University School of Law senior counsel Frederick Schwartz, for example, concluded that expanded powers under former President George W. Bush were the objective of those who believed the post-Watergate reforms hamstrung the President's ability to act on the nation's behalf in times of urgent national security needs.

Other observers might argue that the expansion of executive powers was less of a power grab by the Executive and more of a result of Congressional gridlock. A Council on Foreign Relations report concluded that Congress has hampered its own effectiveness in serving as a check on the President's authorities. The report states that polarization "has politicized the national security arena that, while never immune to partisanship, more often than not, used to bring out the 'country first' instincts in lawmakers."

Gridlock has also enfeebled Congress's role as the legislative body. The 112th Congress (2011-2012) was the least productive Congress from 1947 until its time, having passed less than 2% of the bills introduced, according to

USA Today analysis of records kept by the US House Clerk's office. The Washington Times drew a similar conclusion but additionally measured six separate activities, such as the amount of time each chamber spent officially in session and the number of conference reports written, to create a futility index. According to its analysis in January 2012, the Senate's futility index was the worst it had ever been (70 in 2011 compared to second-worst record of 89 in 2008). The House's futility index was the 10th worst session of the 33 Congresses the study compared. The records of subsequent Congresses until today's 116th are only marginally better.

While Congress's role in determining the law of the land is diminishing, the Judicial Branch appears to be filling the vacuum. Yale and University of California Irvine law professors, William N. Eskridge Jr. and Richard L. Hasen, respectively, explain that historically the Supreme Court would interpret a federal statute but Congress would often override it, or portions of it, with new, related legislation. The overrides enable Congress to nuance legislation to reflect the needs and desires of the American people. Hasen's study reveals that in each two-year term from 1975-1990, Congress overrode an average of 12 Supreme Court decisions. Yet he discovered that the number of overrides fell dramatically to 4.8 from 1990-2000 and then to 2.7 afterward, prompting Professor Pildes of New York University to say that "the court's decisions are likely to be the last word, not the first, on what a statute means." While the long-term implications of the strengthened role of the Supreme Court remain uncertain, Pildes stresses that the downturn in overrides "gives the Supreme Court significantly more power and the Congress significantly less power."

Polarization is clearly changing the roles and balance of power among the three branches of government, and the upheaval is causing confusion across party lines, from activists to passive observers. The changing roles also create two sources of emotional distress: a powerful feeling of the loss of a shared past and a fear of losing control of the future.

When parents divorce, the separation phase creates an immediate sense of the loss of the former family, for children and parents alike. That sense of loss and longing for a return is one of the most emotionally challenging aspects of divorce. Similarly, in polarized America, party loyalists believe they are losing the America they fondly recall. This is not simply whimsical nostalgia. It is real, hard, emotional longing. Georgetown professor E.J. Dionne Jr. believes one reason for this sentiment is that Americans have always debated the government's size and role in either protecting individual rights or creating communal obligations. The Constitution does not explicitly prioritize either individual or community rights, thus those on either side of this debate can and do feel entirely grounded in the Constitution. Dionne suggests much of the current angst America is feeling stems from general disagreement over how the country has balanced these two priorities in the past.

In addition to this sense of loss over the American history each side sees, the parties also fear losing influence over the nation's future. In a divorced family a parent who suddenly loses time with his children worries about also losing their affection. Similarly, political parties view minor compromises and electoral losses as devastating blows to the integrity of "their" America. Every victory on one side represents a degradation of

America to the other side. As parties move to their polar extremes on an extensive range of issues and the stakes of losing appear even more significant, observers like Abramowitz, Sinclair, and Dionne note that the idea of compromise becomes a treasonous concept.

With the spirt of bipartisan compromise evaporating, the distribution of power and control becomes the heart of the issue. For the post-divorce experience to be positive for a family, the emotional turmoil and changing roles produced by physical separation must be replaced with the satisfactory reconstruction of the family. In the political context, this leads directly to phase three, which involves rebuilding America's self-perception by embracing polarization as a reflection of the will of the people and a source of national strength.

Phase Three: Building New Unity
in Polarized America

Divorce expert Constance Ahrons notes that many divorcing couples ask, "How can we get through this without destroying the children? How do we get from this awful place of feeling shattered to some semblance of order?" Americans exhausted from the intensity of polarization may be asking a very similar question: how do we get from this feeling of being a divided nation to one that embraces its differences under an umbrella of unity?

Overcoming polarization's negative consequences requires the participation of the entire range of political actors, from the branches of government to the average voter. Many creative ideas about governmental reforms have been circulating for years for a variety of relatively unrelated reasons. The divorce framework provides a new way of looking at the traditional roles of political actors, potential adjustments necessary to accommodate polarization, and of the central role emotion plays into the establishment of a new and happy normal.

Executive Branch. As the only nationally elected leader, the President's bully pulpit enables him or her to set a powerful example across an expansive range of political activity. Perhaps more than anything else, today's polarized environment requires leadership in active listening and transparent discourse. A President who is willing to dedicate more time to listening to those who oppose him would set an impressive tone of respect by demonstrating concern for the entire population, not just his party. Including members of the opposing party in his Cabinet would be an effective method for a President to create routine opportunities to hear alternatives.

Most Presidents have included only one, if any, opposing party members in their Cabinets. President Obama sought to change that by including three members of the Republican Party in his first Cabinet. It was a start toward arresting one of the trends Doherty notes as undercutting the President's credibility as a unifying national leader.

Ahrons suggest that ex-spouses quickly adjust to the idea that their newly reconstructed family most likely will limit each of them to co-parenting; neither parent should believe he or she has complete control. Divorced parents typically do not divide their children between them. Polarized, two-party politics in America does something very similar. As an elected leader, your constituents include those who did not elect you. American government does not allow for a winner-take-all approach, but rather creates a system that limits party influence to co-influencing. No President can truly claim to have been elected by the majority of American people because no election involved the majority of Americans voting. A President who understands this and sets a consistently respectful tone toward those co-influencing the nation with him could vastly improve his credibility as a national leader.

Legislative Branch. Counseling professors Mark Young and Lynn Long recommend couples in conflict create a joint definition of the problem before debating it. Such advice could be constructive to party activists who routinely use separate news conferences and parallel media outreach to cherry pick aspects of their strategy they want to champion and condemn the perceived flaws in the other party's solutions. Because media outlets and other opinion influencers are increasingly partisan, Americans derive vastly different pictures of the same problem. Thus, there is no shared definition of the problem against which Americans can evaluate the opposing strategies and solutions. Jointly defining problems, rather than blaming problems on the other party, could reduce unhelpful biases associated with particular issues and enable more substantive debate.

For example, if Republicans and Democrats would focus their discussion of Social Security on the original structural flaw of the program, they might succeed in reducing some of the ideological clutter surrounding the debate. Most Americans are probably unaware that when the program began in the 1930s, the life expectancy for men was seven years younger than the age at which

Social Security could initially be collected and three years younger for women. In other words, the authors of the legislation expected most people to be dead well before they would be able to collect the financial safety net. Social Security funds were, therefore, intended for very few people.

Life expectancies by 2015, however, were projected to be ten years beyond the Social Security collection age for men and fifteen years more for women. Political parties can sling blame on each other, but educating Americans on this original structural flaw would go much further toward explaining why the program as originally constructed—without stipulating a collection age pegged to a certain number of years after life expectancy—is unsustainable.

The divorce analogy also offers a model for considering whether new Congressional rules might be appropriate given the new roles emerging from polarization. For example, to improve the likelihood that Congressional leaders understand their district constituents from the opposing party while representing the majority views, Federal election laws could require run-offs when the spread between two candidates does not meet a pre-set threshold. Candidates in a run-off would have to invest more time in understanding where their policies fell short in attracting voters from the middle or the opposing party. Any such compromise positions might then reflect the otherwise disengaged moderate middle or the previously dismissed views of the minority party's following.

Judicial Branch. Because the Supreme Court is focused on the interpretation of law, its range of options for adjusting to the new roles of polarization is limited. Not much has changed in terms of what the Supreme Court does, but its enhanced role in having the final word on legislation magnifies the requirement that Justices approach their review of cases without partisan or personal bias. Organizations like Alliance for Justice note that in today's polarized environment, the external activities and inclinations of a Justice matter. Even if a Justice is able to separate his personal beliefs from his review of a case, any appearance to the contrary weakens public faith in the Court.

Court expert and Visiting Fellow at the Brookings Institution, Russell Wheeler suggests making the Supreme Court more accountable to a standard set of ethics but admits that for a code to be effective, it requires an enforcement mechanism. The U.S. Constitution explicitly created one Supreme Court, meaning there is no natural body to review complaints or punish infractions by Supreme Court Justices. On the other hand, Wheeler argues that because Justices have occasionally noted they refer to the Judicial Code of Conduct for ethical guidance, they should at least publicize what guidelines they use to enhance the transparency of the Court.

In the end, the only oversight or checks and balances of the Supreme Court are the people. The people can demand that their legislators table new laws to chip away at a Supreme Court decision. The role of the free press is critical in keeping the decisions of the Supreme Court transparent.

Party leaders, activists, and candidates. Party leaders and activists are at the critical juncture between the passive majority of the population, who may rely on cues from this active cadre to shape voting preferences, and the leaders in office who carry out the responsibilities of governance. This intersection gives party activists a unique ability to influence both leaders and followers. How they behave, therefore, is a key indicator of whether the nation is rebuilding unity or further tearing itself apart.

Polarization is creating cookie-cutter candidates, and one of the most significant steps parties could take would be to modify nomination processes explicitly to diversify their pool of prospects. Cloned candidates may be leaving a large block of voters, whose views are not as ideologically cohesive, unrepresented. But given Sinclair and Abramowitz's portrait of the eroding middle, why would parties risk changing nomination practices that produce predictable candidates? Since parties presumably are always seeking strategies for increasing votes, diverse candidates may develop new or nuanced positions that have been untested due to complacency, but that better reflect party loyalists. Such positions also could attract new voters and increase margins of victory.

Other actors. Closer to the grassroots level are a host of other actors who can shape America's future approach to polarization. Within this group are the nongovernmental organizations, think tanks, and traditional and social media outlets that grew more partisan as America polarized. These institutions can elevate the debate when they adhere to methodical research and critical thinking. Doing so does not require them to abandon their partisan attachments, but enables them to inspire innovative thinking that might be outside the box for party insiders. Provided these organizations resist the temptation to pander to party lines, their services are considerable in fulfilling the need for transparency in democratic governance and the education of the electorate.

Grassroots. Given the general population's lack of knowledge about the basics of the US government, the average voter is unlikely to participate in rekindling unity in America unless it is better informed. If many Americans are unaware of the existence of the three branches of government, they most likely view anti-majoritarian practices, such as longer Senate terms, lifetime appointments of Supreme Court Justices, and the filibuster, as obscure and inconsequential. While understanding the details of the system of checks and balances is key to adapting in a polarized America, the National Constitution Center's survey suggests Americans have a lot of homework. The activism of citizens, and especially the enthusiasm of the youth, is indispensable in engaging and educating the electorate.

America's Good Divorce: Embracing Political Duality as Key to Unity

The first step toward the reconstruction of a family is for the members of it to define what they want it to be. Ahron argues that divorce has been stigmatized unfairly by society. She warns against assuming divorces are the tragic destruction of a family and recommends society see that divorce often is the welcome reconstruction of family that had become seriously unhealthy.

Divorce does not eradicate the existence of all family relationships. She further argues that despite all the changes that occur with the physical separation, the basic purpose of the binuclear family remains the same as it was for the nuclear family: to nurture and love, provide security, and enable happiness for each family member. Sounds a bit like Life, Liberty, and the Pursuit of Happiness.

Many years after a marital divorce, the wedding of one of the children may be less than idyllic for ex-spouses, yet participating as ex-spouses is far better for both parents and the child than missing the momentous occasion altogether. The experience will be less than perfect for all, but should not be disastrous to any. My co-parent and I share birthdays and graduations without issues. The focus for both of us has always been, and remains, celebrating our children. When they give him a huge hug or go eat a celebratory lunch with him, I am happy. My children need, want, and deserve a wonderful relationship with their father as much as they do with me. We both know that they need and want to love us both, and it is not a competition. We have to let go of control and allow them to become adults. That is what selfless love of your children requires. Neither my former spouse nor I wish to ever become impostures of pretended parental love.

Ultimately, in a post-polarized America, the goal is similar. Republicans and Democrats from all walks of life will want to participate in rebuilding America after its time-out, and after every time it suffers. Demonstrating restraint and respectfulness will make the experience less than ideal to each side because it requires compromise, but to be left out of America's experience entirely would be a disaster for all.

As with my personal experience, we may not be a nuclear family in America anymore, but we remain a family. If every American took a DNA test, they may be surprised to find how blended we all truly are. I was thrilled to discover that my own family history is far more eclectic than the stories I heard from grandparents. I am not half of anything even though some family members did immigrate rather recently. I have a fascinating mixture of European, African, and Eurasian history. I now proudly consider myself an all-American artisan blend. I am American.

We are family. Americans remain tied to each other and to each other's fate despite the distancing of their political views because we still belong to each other. We are children of the Constitution and its idea of America. One of the most significant ways we can rebuild and strengthen our family is to commit to tolerance of political dissent—to see tolerance as our most enduring and endless source of unifying strength.

"A house divided against itself cannot stand."
— ABRAHAM LINCOLN

VOICES OF AMERICAN WOMEN

#9

Essay by Alexis

My name is Alexis. Growing up, I was always surrounded by the idea of being a part of something "bigger than yourself," mainly because my father was a captain in the Army, which had a significant impact on me. I was so proud to be the daughter of a soldier, the fighter for a free America. He was my hero. Though my interest in being involved in national security issues did not immediately stem from my father's service, the idea that I held, would eventually carry me there. That idea, the connection to something greater than myself, and several years of reading collections of history books, would lead to my passion to become an avid participant in US National Security.

In school, American and World history were always my favorite subjects. US military history and the relations between the US and the rest of the world really drew me in. I would read my AP American History textbook at home in my spare time, skipping ahead in all the lessons, which is when I discovered and became immersed in learning about Cold War history. I constantly found and asked for book recommendations about anything Cold War related and would sometimes search government agencies' websites for declassified files and case studies for that time.

Learning about these events in the past engaged my interest in how significant historical events impacted the lives of Americans then, and now. The books slowly transitioned from the Cold War and Soviet-Afghan War to the attacks on 9/11, the wars in Afghanistan and Iraq, and the impact 9/11 had on American society and the world; this would ignite my spark and passion to some-day work in the national security arena.

I was no stranger to the events of 9/11. Though I cannot tell you where I was or what I was doing in that exact moment when America would soon learn it had been a victim of terrorism once again, I can still tell you how it impacted and shaped my world. My father went to fight in the invasion of Iraq in 2003 as part of Opera-tion Iraqi Freedom (OIF1), and the capturing of Saddam Hussein. As I read my books about 9/11 and events after, I began to take a closer look regarding how these events affected, and continue to affect, our national security polices today. I began to understand that Americans' sense of physical security was shattered by the attacks on 9/11. I learned how it shifted our nation's attitudes about safety, which intensified the US national security and defense strategies. The 9/11 attack and the resulting "War on Terror" shaped the America I grew up in.

I continued to study current events and terrorist organizations involved in the Middle East, Northern Africa, the Horn of Africa, and how the US responded to such organizations and events. Dedicated to my passion of being involved in national security, after I graduated high school I decided to join the US Army Reserves as a Psychological Operations Specialist, while also majoring in international studies with a focus on security and intelligence. Being in the Army has allowed me to get my foot in the door and become involved in national security from a defensive perspective, while also gaining real-world experience firsthand. My military experience, coupled with my education, will help me not only learn about the changing nature of conflict and war, but also to participate in the experience and not just learn the theory. US national security is something I believe everyone should be interested in. It is the protection of America, its citizens, economy, and the institutions under which we are united, from foreign or internal organizations that wish to threaten our liberties.

I am at the very beginning of my journey to a career in national security. Through these early stages, I have noticed that the world of national security is constantly shifting and changing based on current policies and events. National security is not a straightforward or simple conversation to have, which can make the process of learning a bit hard. However, do not let this deter you from a career or interest in national security, but rather let it inspire you to engage in those difficult conversations. And if you think something is difficult, I ask you to remember this:

"Do not think that what is hard for you to master is humanly impossible; but if a thing is humanly possible, consider it to be within your reach."
— MARCUS AURELIUS

VOICES OF AMERICAN WOMEN

#10

National Security and Me

Essay by Erin Connolly, Girl Security Board Adviser

One of my earliest childhood memories is sitting in my first grade classroom on a sunny morning in 2001. Even as a six-year-old, I noticed a shift in the mood soon after the first bell rang. More and more friends were being picked up from school before we even made it to recess. I became increasingly worried as I waited to see if my mom would also come. Eventually my name was called over the loudspeaker and I found her. She had the same worried look all adults seemed to share that morning. We drove home and I learned that something terrible had occurred just an hour away. Yet, in the midst of the chaos and tragedy, I never questioned my own personal security.

As I progressed through school, I became increasingly aware of my own personal security—or the lack thereof. Lockdown drills, active shooter drills, and bomb threats served as reminders of my constant vulnerability. While practice can add to security in a real crisis, I was never quite convinced crouching away from a window would save me and my classmates. Nonetheless, we went through the motions to avoid detention.

In college, I became acutely aware of my personal security. The constant warnings: never walk home alone, make sure to get your own drink, text friends if you are meeting someone new, all reminded me that I alone could not meet my security needs. Friends would provide "back up" in case anyone ever needed an escape plan, and this was just on a protected college campus. We never confronted community violence on a larger scale, but even within the college bubble I was always aware of how easily I could lose control over my own body. Resilience remained a critical and common trait among myself and my female peers. My personal security was a consistent background concern as I studied national security policy in the classroom.

Upon graduation, I moved to Washington, DC, the place where policy is made and I could focus on international concerns, on issues greater than myself. While I dove into policy, I noticed my personal security was never completely secured. I still walk home with my keys in my hand, check on friends to make sure they get home okay, not only ward off unwanted advances at the bar, but also in my field.

Being a woman in national security policy is frustrating, and this is only amplified by the need to explain why it is so frustrating. Why do I need to explain that my ideas have merit, why is being "friendly" conflated with wanting to date, why do I need to "earn" the right to be sarcastic in written work? I had grown accustomed to the mental work of securing my safety in public, but the mental work of securing my position in a field many assume I do not belong *is* an adjustment. Some could say I did not adjust well since I really did not adjust at all.

I do not think I need to explain why my ideas have just as much merit as my male peers', why my being nice to a colleague has nothing to do with romantic interest, and why I have the right to my own written voice. I found that the issues permeating my daily activities contribute to broader national security challenges.

Growing up with the constant concern for personal security widens the solution set in life. I learned how to defuse tension, mitigate conflict, stick up for myself when necessary, and sometimes just walk away. Decisions are based on what will not pose an additional risk to my—or my friend's—security. Impulsive reactions often appeal to me in the moment, but I learned to take a breath before taking action. To be resilient even when I want to be reactionary. Aggression towards an already confrontational person usually further escalates and ultimately undermines my own security. It's hard to recognize that sometimes my first impulse is actually harmful to myself, but because I immediately felt the repercussions of an impulsive decision I learned to be less reactionary and more deliberate.

The American national security establishment has yet to fully grapple with the impact of reactionary versus deliberate decision-making. In a space largely defined and dominated by those who historically have fewer personal security concerns, aggression may present a logical path forward. We have somehow avoided realizing how asserting dominance over another person or country does not automatically benefit the aggressor. While reacting "strongly" temporarily creates a sense of security, a feeling of control, and seems as though we have stabilized a situation, it is not a sustainable approach. Aggression is reactionary, and while it is at times appropriate, it can also undermine strategic objectives. The aggressive approach is also becoming less viable as conflict moves from traditional to increasingly borderless threats. American national security is utterly unprepared.

America is unprepared for, but not incapable of, adjusting to the evolving national security environment. The United States has demonstrated unique strength in the face of hardship, as demonstrated post-9/11. Our country united and demonstrated compassion for one another during an incredibly difficult time. While we supported the troops and initial war effort, public interest quickly waned to the point where many Americans do not even realize we are still at war. Support for initial action has faded into complacency. While such a tragedy merited a response, there has been no critical examination of the path chosen. Instead, our initial reaction in Afghanistan quickly spiraled into an invasion of Iraq, six trillion dollars, and the longest war in our history.

As threats change and the definition of national security continues to adapt, it is critical that the United States learn to examine reactions, evaluate effective responses, and reflect on decisions. While not an easy task, an inclusive and diverse group of decision makers will facilitate a new era of resilient national security that can withstand emerging threats, and we can move beyond lockdown drills.

Step 4:
Ending America's Time-Out

After some time has passed and your child is calm, you likely will want to end the time-out and have a conversation with your child about her future behavior. But first, there is the all-important warmth and unspoken love that comes from reaching out with a comforting embrace, or gentle pat on the head or back, so that your troubled child knows that she is still loved by you. Sometimes this is harder to do when you have been hurt by your child's behavior or rants. But the physical connection creates an emotional bond, and the healing instantly begins.

America has some hard reaching out to do. Opposing sides of all stripes—parties, gender, race, ethnicities, religion, age—must swallow their pride and extend a hand as well as calm their words. What might this handshake look like?

A Democratic activist walking up to a Republican activist at a polling place and offering a cup of coffee and saying, "Thanks for serving."

A woman turning to the man who holds the door for her and saying thanks, because it was an act of kindness, not disempowerment.

A first-generation immigrant offering a smile to a protestor and asking if he can share his family's story so the protestors understand how hard it is to access the American Dream.

A Muslim or Hindu asking a Christian or Jew to discuss mutual goals for overcoming destructive climate change as a demonstration of respect for the god that entrusted the blessings of earth to mankind.

A Baby Boomer on the Board of Directors setting up a reverse mentoring program to allow the senior executives to learn from Millennials.

A young white male, who sees his future being chipped away by affirmative action policies that he perceives give others an advantage over him, realizing that his hard-earned merit was borne from opportunities he and his family were given for the color of their skin.

A young African-American woman, who is forever being subjected to a culture of tokenism, sharing her skillsets and talents with non-minorities without fearing she will be devalued afterward.

Some brilliant engineers and scientists dedicating their passion into building technologies that create unbiased solutions to conflicts rather than enable war to be easier, deadlier, and more automated.

This is how we can connect the better dots and create an image of America that is strong and ideal. Yes, it will be hard. As noted American poet John Greenleaf Whittier said in the 1800s, "Peace hath higher tests of manhood than battle ever knew." But today America will also draw on the strength of women and children to extend the hand of peace with empathy. This may require putting a hold on the instinct for justice when you are reaching out to those who have wronged you. But it is not the same thing as giving forgiveness or forgetting the injustice done to you. It is a recognition that you, the wronged, are the one with the power to create change.

In urging Americans to rededicate themselves to adherence to the Constitution, Abraham Lincoln argued that, "Reason, cold, calculating, unimpassioned reason, must furnish all the materials for our future support and defense. Upon these let the proud fabric of freedom rest."

With no disrespect to Lincoln, America's emotional fabric has been ripped by the "four horsemen of the Apocalypse" of our pre-divorce polarized country. Reason alone is not going to heal us, especially while we are still flinging insults and injury at each other and being exploited by foreign detractors. We need emotional healing. And this is why a time-out is so appropriate.

A child will never act rationally while still raging with anger. Only after the quiet of her time-out, will she feel the tug of wanting to show she can be better. Nothing reopens a heart more fully than the exhaustion of rage, followed by the vulnerability of remorse.

Chapter 7

Ending the Battle of the Sexes

How do we hit the reset button when Americans are still kicking and screaming at each other? How can we as individuals get to the place of wanting America to behave better if we are still arguing, particularly about social and gender equality?

What is it that we tell our children when they are being bullyish or purposefully excluding another child from a game? "Try to put yourself in her shoes" or "Imagine how you would feel if all the boys left you out of the game." When we tell our children this, we are not just teaching them how to be kind and patient with other kids, we are also subtly teaching them the profound importance of empathy. Empathy is a critical emotional intelligence tool for enabling our hearts to go where our minds are unfamiliar.

Even with adult children, I still have teaching moments because it is hard to lead with your heart when your brain, and your hardwired biases perceive a threat. For example, my son encountered a "threat" while at college when he was interning with the local police as a criminal justice major. A group of students were gathered to protest the Administration's immigration policy outside the local police station. Someone aggressively approached my son and accused him of being a nazi. My son kept his cool, but he called me later very upset and said, "Mom, how could he just look into my face and decide what I was? He doesn't know me. He'd never met me." We had a long talk about the biases we build up in our heads over time. I reminded him to consider how it might feel as a young African-American girl always being presumed to be something she is not, or worse, less than she is. He understood, and I believe was able to turn an unpleasant experience into an opportunity to build more empathy.

It is important to remember that the bad people of this world are far fewer in number than the good people. After three decades of countering terrorism, I still believe this. This is the faith in humanity that I have raised my children to believe in, too. I remind them that when they are identifying those who have wronged them, it's worth taking a breath to remember the many, many more who may look and sound the same, but who are not the same. They are not your enemies, unless you make them so.

Over the decades of my involvement in counterterrorism, I have observed how hard it is to believe this. Terrorists steal the legitimacy of aggrieved populations struggling to have their cause addressed. When that happens, the world tends to ignore the legitimate needs of the peaceful community out of fear of appeasing the terrorists. No one wants to acknowledge that the terrorists have disproportionate impact on society because that would be perceived as validating their self-enhanced stature. But what happens as a result of this good intention? Legitimate needs go unaddressed, and the aggrieved population must also fend off the terrorists themselves. Most importantly, the irony is by not making efforts to alleviate the grievances that both the peaceful population and the terrorists call attention to, those who refuse to "give into terrorists" have done just that. They give up their independence of action by giving into the fear of how it would appear.

We are doing this within America. We are presuming that when we have been wronged by someone, that the much, much larger community of people who look or sound like our aggressor is going to wrong us, too. We hunker down and protect ourselves by refusing to listen. Or worse, we strike first, out of fear of losing. This is a cycle of prejudice and hatred that becomes self-fulfilling.

These self-perpetuating cycles are occurring across a number of issues in America. When we equate someone's political affiliation with evil, we have created a self-fulfilling cycle of hatred. When we treat someone's religion as an existential threat to our own, we have created enemies rather than opening our hearts to fellow children of God. When we degrade another human being because of the color of their skin, accent, size, clothing, music, culture, or age, we are creating enemies when we could be expanding the strength of our citizenry. When we treat all men as if they were responsible for sexual violence, harassment, and discrimination against girls and women, we are missing an opportunity to change our world through collaboration.

How do we break these cycles? Digging deep and growing our empathy skills.

I am waiting for augmented virtual reality to enable a man to experience what it is like living a day as a girl. Or for a white woman to live a day as a woman of color and a Democrat to live the life of a Republican, etc. To experience another person's every moment of being judged by their appearance or identity is illuminating.

Nothing can build empathy like that. But if we can tap the imaginations of our childhood and try, it's what we have until the gamers of the world see the value in such educational programming.

Imagine you enter a room and don virtual reality goggles and then experience an ordinary day in the life of someone you oppose or do not understand. You might find it surprising what you learn.

Once suited up, the man enters the room and is transformed into a 14-year old girl. Here are some of the experiences to be expected:

- Fear from start to finish. Your anxiety will begin when you choose clothes for school. Too plain, and the boys will think you are boring and the girls will think you are out of touch with today's fashion. Too fashionable and you are bound to be considered as trying to dress sexy, since fashion idolizes sex and sensuality. Will you risk a dress code violation or social alienation?

- In your science class, the teacher will tell you to let your male lab partner light the fire on your Bunsen burner. No explanation necessary because your teacher assumes that boys know more about handling fire.

- When the boys at lunch tell you that you should be a stripper, you are not allowed to be offended. You must smile and act as if you've been compli- mented. Even your school vice-principal has told you that you are pretty and must learn how to expect that kind of attention from boys.

- When you hear the same group of boys joking and laughing about what they'd like to see you take off first in this imaginary strip club they've created for you, you have to continue to ignore it. The girls next to you will tell you that you are lucky they even notice you, and the teacher will merely brush it off as poorly constructed attempts to flatter you.

- Just smile, do your work, and don't pay any attention to them. It's just "locker room" talk.

- On the way to the locker room for gym class, you are approached by this boy and his friend. There is no one else around and you immediately feel vulnerable. The one boy starts making cliché stripper music while the other pretends to offer dollar bills to get you to take your shirt off. You tell them to stop and that it's not funny and they just laugh. They also move in closer. You panic and push one of them away and run to the girls locker room.

- You dress for gym in a uniform that does not fit you at all because it is of course a boy's uniform. As all school gym uniforms are for some reason. Your sides and thighs chafe from sweating and the bulky fabric irritating your skin. You will be ridiculed for your inability to shoot the ball straight even though you can do a back flip on a balance beam. When the humiliation is over, you will hear the same boys who were taunting you earlier claim there is a hidden camera in the girls locker room for them to watch you and your friends. Even though you know they are teasing, you change quickly into your clothes.

- By the time the school day is over, you just want to be home in your room listening to music and done with your homework. But, the boys are following you to your bus. They sit behind you and tell you that you should never have pushed them in the hallway. Then they restart their taunting about your clothes and insinuate that because you are sweaty, you should want to take off your clothes.

- As your bus stop gets closer, you dig around in your backpack for anything sharp or long that you could wield to keep them from getting too close to you. But the bus stops too soon and you have to get off. Of course, they follow you.

- As you descend the stairs, you feel a hand grab your shoulder.

The employee at this virtual reality station tells you your time is up. A good thing for you because what you do not realize as you revert back to the man you really are is that the young girl whose reality you assumed for a brief time is about to successfully escape the boys who were taunting her all day, only to be molested by her uncle in her own home.

Women have no choice but to *expect* to have their physical integrity threatened or violated during their lifetime. Women are socialized from a very young age—if they are fortunate not to be abused—to be profoundly aware of their physical vulnerability. As girls, we are trained to be afraid and to be in tune with the possibility of threat at every corner, but most especially inside our own homes, schools, and neighborhoods. What's worse is that we grow up with a justice sector and societal norms that ignore or even normalize sexual abuse against us.

Men, can you imagine living in constant fear like that? Can you imagine being sexually harassed or assaulted throughout your lifetime and having everyone around you dismiss it and objectify you without thinking twice about it? What would you do if they tell you that you are making too big a deal of it, or that you should smile more, or that you are to blame based on what you wore? And in the same breath, society and advertising are telling you that you need to look sexier, all the time, or else women will never be interested in you.

At the age of six, girls are no longer believed to be as smart as boys. Men, can you imagine growing up almost your whole life believing that no one, including yourself, believes you are as smart as girls?

Justice Ginsberg said, "Women belong in all places where decisions are being made." Women have been, and still are, routinely excluded from the places where decisions are made: from schools and businesses, hospitals and universities, to local city councils and the White House. Men, can you imagine being excluded from making decisions with your brain for no other reason than the form of your reproductive system? Or how about if you are able to muscle your way into the female-dominated boardrooms of America, only to learn that you will earn at best 80% of a woman's salary doing the same work?

Men, can you imagine living in a world today where the entire history of everything—the basic concepts and constructs created around power, religion, health, money, politics, and technology are all entirely female derived? What if you try to challenge history's ignorance of you, only to be told that you are being unreasonable or irrational? Or too emotional?

I remember having a fascinating exchange about

whether women could make good football coaches and managers if they have never played football. I asked the question why is determining the potential for coaching a sport dependent upon having played the sport? Surely there are other ways to determine effective coaching skills and knowledge? For a very long time, only men were allowed to be doctors and surgeons. That includes doctors who provided healthcare for pregnant women and delivered their babies. Why were men presumed to be capable of controlling a life-threatening activity that they had never experienced? Or more importantly, why did men never question their competency to manage a life-or-death process that they will never experience? And most importantly, why were women denied the right to question the competency of those male doctors while men can question the competency of a woman to coach a sport she has not played?

Welcome men, to a world of being presumed you are "not." Not smart enough, not strong enough, not capable enough, not savvy enough, not fast enough, not stoic enough, not brave enough, not there, not, not, not. It is exhausting to live with having to justify every aspect about yourself. Everywhere a woman turns, anything that is based on a human being is based on a man—from the height of your toilet to the size of your desk chair or from the nutritional labels on your food to the definition of justice, equality, and security.

The #MeToo Movement is focused on sexual assault, harassment, and discrimination. But the underlying condition that has enabled this problem to remain so widespread, is the ubiquitous legacy of history's acceptance of misogyny. What men may find hard to understand is that so much of the deep anger felt among so many women does not come from their thinking every man is a predator or that every clumsy compliment is harassment, but stems from the lack of men who are willing to acknowledge misogyny's destructive legacy and help us break it.

America, our children, indeed the world, needs the battle of the sexes to end. It's time for empathy and conversations. Both men and women need to have the courage to say, "I would like to better understand you. Please share your experiences with me."

VOICES OF AMERICAN WOMEN

#11

Essay on gender roles in ethics by Emily Burchfield, Masters Candidate, Security Studies Program, Edmund A. Walsh School of Foreign Service, Georgetown University

The thing that surprised me most about creating and solving an ethical dilemma in a team environment was the role that gender played in the process.

The women in my group voiced their opinions during the creation of the dilemma, offering perspectives that enhanced, rather than distracted from, the discussion of ethics. For example, women were particularly perceptive about the tensions in the "justice versus mercy" paradigm in the dilemma we created, and more sensitive to the considerations of care-based ethics in the dilemma we solved. The women in my group, myself included, tended to be more naturally empathetic to the feelings of all parties involved in the dilemmas, and factored that into the ethical discussion. For example, in the dilemma we created that debated the ethics of giving a "golden parachute" to a dictator responsible for mass slaughter of civilians, the women in our group were more attentive to the consequences of not addressing—and perhaps exacerbating—the grievances of the population.

This I suppose was not too surprising to me, as previous experience has suggested that women can contribute empathy and understanding to discussions of national security, ethical or otherwise. What surprised me more was witnessing how even when external barriers to women's participation are reduced, internalized gender barriers can still be difficult to overcome. In our group, women actually outnumbered men three to two, and we operated with the knowledge that our work would be reviewed by a woman in a position of power. This is not representative of the national security apparatus, and the difference did empower women to voice their opinions. However, one experience was remarkable to me. At the end of a round of vigorous, yet respectful, ethical discussion, in which the women in the group spoke their minds freely, one of them turned to the rest of us and said, "Why do I feel like such a bitch right now?"

Another woman in the group responded that she had a similar feeling of discomfort with perhaps having "said too much," and apologized. These strong, smart, successful women were essentially saying sorry for speaking their minds. It surprised me, although, I guess I really shouldn't be surprised. Women have been taught for centuries to be quiet, demure, and deferential to the opinions of men. Those who dare to do things differently are frequently ridiculed for being "shrill," "bossy," and, yes, "bitchy." And the punishment of women who choose to participate in public affairs—not just those related to national security—is not limited to words: it manifests in unequal pay and promotion, discriminatory policies, and sexual harassment. There's a reason it's a little scary for a girl to speak her mind.

Of course women have internalized these things. It makes sense that even the most educated and empowered can feel some discomfort engaging in an ethical debate. It shouldn't have surprised me, but it did, and I guess that's a good thing. I want to live in a world where it would be *truly shocking* for women to restrain or doubt themselves while engaging in any kind of debate. I believe that the more women participate in these types of discussion and support others doing so, the more our national *and* personal security will be improved.

VOICES OF AMERICAN WOMEN

#12

A letter from the author's journal

Dear Journal,

I want to tell you about the most extraordinary thing that happened to me while I was in Sun Valley. I was attending a conference about amazing women who have changed so many lives and the face of America. This experience fundamentally changed me, too.

You need to know that for over forty years, there was a demon in my soul. Like a monster gripping my entire insides, I was imprisoned inside myself. My gremlins—those default behaviors that controlled every aspect of my life by deciding how I would act, react, and interact to every situation and every person—were but servants to this larger devil. Every time I lashed out at a gremlin, the monster was there to bolster it. Every time I felt my small inner voice speak up, the monster was there amplifying my gremlins chattering at me, always shutting the real me out. The noise inside my head was deafening. I could never find quiet. There was never any peace.

The more I struggled to free myself of these gremlins one at a time, the more the monster fought back. My gremlins told me that I needed them to survive. That I would come undone altogether if I stopped listening to them. They told me that they had gotten me this far, through hard times. They told me this is who I was, and I had to accept it.

I did accept it for decades. But then for a short time, I was loved by someone. I felt love like I had never experienced it before. I felt loved and I had the ability to love. I had never known this. I had never truly experienced trust and willful surrender, only fear and fighting. Once I had a taste of this new feeling, I could not go back to my old self. But my monster was dictating my behaviors and undermining my new relationship.

I knew I had to purge myself of this devil and destroy the grip it had on me. I was no longer okay with being someone who no one could love. But I had no idea how to identify this amorphous beast inside my soul. The only thing I could do was what I had avoided my whole life. My only way forward was to go back, to think back and recount in my own head everything that I had experienced, and accept that it happened.

So I went back to my childhood. I let the memories flood my mind. I did not shut them out. I let them in, and they were horrible. I saw the little girl who suffered so much betrayal and pain. I saw her holding her breath. I saw her screaming silently until it stopped. I saw her wishing she could die and escape the grotesqueness. She screamed at me, begging me to make it stop. But I just watched. I did not try to rescue her. I did nothing to try to save her. I did nothing but watch and pity her. I knew what she was suffering and yet, I did nothing. She was desperate for a way out, but there was no way out. And I watched. I hated myself because I knew what this poor little girl was suffering and still I froze and did nothing.

That was the devil in me. The grown woman who could not accept that she did nothing to save the little girl who she was, who could not forgive herself for failing to find a way to escape the abuse. The adult version of me who could not believe that as a child, there was nothing more I could have done to stop it. The devil in me gripping my heart, soul, mind, and body was shame. This was the monster that I so badly wanted to shake out. But knowing what it was brought me no relief. I felt only more hopelessness because I had no idea how to destroy this demon. For months, I had resigned myself to a life of battling the gremlins that I could never kill because the devil would always resuscitate them after every one of my blows.

Until an entirely unexpected moment in Sun Valley exposed the critical vulnerability in my devil and a way to finally destroy it.

It was a powerful moment. I saw it in his face. The honesty and the passion of the moment. I saw it in the full focus of his eyes as he looked through my skin—my wall—and right into the soul I had felt for so long was dark and distorted. I heard the power of absolute conviction in his voice when he said, "Gina, I love you." I was not a hideous demon to him. I was an ethereal spirit inspiring liberation, not mine but his. It was in his voice and it was in his face. I was strong with a beautiful soul to him.

And then I felt it in his warm, full embrace. When he scooped up my small body into his huge arms, I did not feel hideous or small. I felt like a Winged Victory, beautiful, invincible and strong. No longer overshadowed by a hideous demon. The monster that had so long gripped my body, soul, mind, and heart was lifted from me just as he so easily lifted me to meet his huge heart with his great big Texan hug.

I will never be the same. Thanks to the courage and warmth of a stranger sitting in an audience listening to me speak, I was given the weapon I needed to destroy the devil—unconditional, unlimited, and freely given acceptance of me. The grace and beauty of that generous gift undid all the agony of that hideous demon. My gremlins have no monster to shelter them. I am on the attack. They will lose. And my battle is my dance. And so I dance and no one can stop me. And I dance every day without the devil on my back. I dance with my optimism. I dance with my kindness. I dance with my strength and with my beauty. And I will never stop dancing.

Chapter 8

Women's Work Is Governance

Simone de Beauvoir wrote, "Representation of the world, like the world itself, is the work of men: they describe it from their own point of view, which they confuse with the absolute truth."

World history, politics, science, literature—all recorded nearly exclusively by men have also all drawn nearly exclusively from the male experience. What were the women doing while the Greeks were philosophizing and creating democracies? While Roman legions were conquering the world? While the Founding Fathers were writing the Declaration of Independence?

The 1966 University of Chicago symposium, "Man the Hunter" concluded that evolution in hunting was central to human evolution and development. There was very little dispute of this finding at the time, or even today. Most people—men and women—will read that sentence without much concern. The evolution in hunting from hands to tools, from individually to groups, and the development of methods and measures to make it safer and sustainable over time all seem like central evolutionary behaviors to the many industries of today, such as infrastructure building and national defense.

This is precisely the male absolute that de Beauvoir referred to. The implication throughout history that defining all human adaptation as stemming from the male experience is not okay. This default, and perhaps even more so the acceptance of it without question by men or women, eradicates the equal importance of the adaptation of the female experience.

This default is also the foundation upon which misogyny as a political construct continues to rest. "Man the Hunter" imbues a biased theory of evolution—one that considers only half of humankind—in scientific fact. In defining primacy and dominance in terms that derive from physical attributes of early humans, "Man the Hunter" diminishes the significance of the adaptive capabilities of human intellect, psychology, and emotion, regardless of gender. The normalizing of "Man the Hunter" created a culture that prioritizes violence as both a means and an end. "Man the Hunter" normalizes sexual predation. "Man the Hunter" ultimately establishes misogyny as part of natural law by extending the physical dominance of men to intellectual, societal, and governing dominance without questioning the evidentiary base of the linkage.

Anthropologist Sally Slocum challenged the entire premise of "Man the Hunter" with her article, "Woman the Gatherer." Women were responsible for gathering resources to feed large families and communities in collaboration. They needed to know which foods were nutritious and which were dangerous. They developed the skills to predict growth patterns of their community and future needs based on seasons, climate, and topography. They had to teach children how to thrive and be self-sufficient. Women were not threat focused, but cooperation focused.

As women continued to adapt their cooperation-focused responsibilities and roles, they learned management skills that enable multitasking and decision-making on grand scales that had life and death consequences for the many children under their care. Doesn't that sound like managing a community? Or a nation? Women prioritized teaching values and foundational skills because they had to ensure the peacefulness of the human race. Wouldn't you think that the adaptation of women might be important to explaining the history of the human race?

"Woman the Gatherer" was profoundly different from "Man the Hunter." Yet, history's equating of the human experience and priorities with the experience of "Man the Hunter" created a global default toward physical might, threat, and defense as the most important forms of power. This is true in and outside the political sphere.

German philosopher Max Weber's characterization of a modern state as a "human community that (successfully) claims the monopoly of the legitimate use of physical force within a given territory" underscores this point. Moreover, the universality of his definition as the first and last word on statehood demonstrates the extent to which all political definitions are ingrained in "Man the Hunter" concepts. Weber narrows it all down to turf and might. And while turf and might may matter a great deal, so does heart and soul.

"Woman the Gatherer" might say that a state is, "a community that (successfully) claims the monopoly on the execution of justice for all to thrive."

Because women around the world do an average of 79% of the unpaid work—such as raising children—it may be that men have not had the opportunity or the inclination to learn what mothers know: that it takes serious work to foster a well-behaved child. Raising children has long been thought to be "women's work." And in many countries and among many people in America, it still is. This is not the point, though. Just because it has been, or even is, "women's work," does not make it irrelevant beyond the home or beyond the family. This work of women is profoundly critical to making a well-behaved nation and a stable, peaceful world. And yet, "women's work" is routinely treated as irrelevant in politics, security, and international relations when it can arguably be viewed as equally central to governance as the adaptation of hunting.

The inclusion of women in the work of fostering communities, villages, towns, cities, states, and nations—via political leadership—is increasing. While women engaging in political leadership are required to learn about the male conceptual frameworks for politics, security, and international relations because they are the assumed default, are men embracing the opportunity to realize that there are other concepts?

The "work of women" has been disregarded as having relevance outside the home for millennia, but this fact of history does not make the argument correct. Look at all the skills required to lead in a political arena, not the skills to defend it, and ask yourself how similar they are to the skills required to be a parent. A mother takes on the responsibilities of gathering resources to enable her children to be independent and capable adults. Those resources are not limited to material ones but include intellectual and emotional skills to cope with the difficulties of life and to thrive. Those are the leadership traits the world's nations could really use.

Yet, in a world of 195 countries, only 10% have a female head of state. If we were in a world with 90% of the nations led by women, I bet men would be arguing for inclusion of their concepts into politics, and rightly so, because we do have to consider physical aspects of power, threats, and defense.

Study after study concludes that the inclusion of women in politics and the workforces of countries improves the country's well-being, from the economy to security and health. For example, countries with higher participation of women in the labor force exhibit lower levels of international violence and are less likely to use military force to resolve international conflict. Put another way, countries with only 10% of women in the workforce compared to countries with 40% are 30 times more likely to experience internal conflict, according to the World Bank.

Gender equality also correlates with a nation's security and stability, especially when women are involved in governance. Countries benefit from the issues that women have a stronger tendency to prioritize, such as education, health, and family life. It would seem the impact of the adaptation of "woman the gatherer" to nurture, nourish, and guide by gathering resources is innate. It is just as powerful as the male instinct to defend and protect turf by establishing physical dominance. Families, communities, societies, and nations need both.

There are countless studies in the United States, too, that demonstrate women bring balance to business and improve both effectiveness and profitability. Women understand and reach markets that men don't. Women identify problems that historically go unseen. Women offer creativity and innovation that the traditional way of doing business does not. And the result is greater effectiveness, profitability, and happier workforces. More and more studies link greater gender diversity in executive positions with the financial success of those businesses.

Gender diversity improves the bottom line of any business just as it is empirically proven to correlate with nation-level stability, security, and economic growth. This should be a powerful and obvious reason for embracing the role of women in leadership and management where they can make strategic-level decisions that improve both job satisfaction across the whole workforce and the bottom line for the company.

Despite growing data supporting the inclusion of women in every place that decisions are being made, women continually confront a pervasive mindset anchored in historical definitions, standards, and expectations against which every aspect of their performance is measured. These definitions, standards, and expectations are the result of the fact of history that men created them in their own image.

But being a "fact" of history does not make something right. It is a fact of history that the world was flat. It is a fact of history that "blowing smoke up your ass" actually meant using a tobacco smoke enema to cure you of a headache or other illness. It is a fact of history that men once used electric shock therapy directly to their genitals to "cure" impotence.

I believe the argument once used to break women into the workforce—that the work of most industries is gender neutral—was fundamentally flawed. I understand why the argument was used by the women of the Baby Boomer generation to create the conditions for women in fields once thought the sole domain of men. But we continue to be frustrated by the inability of women to reach parity at leadership levels. The glass ceiling still exists. Why?

Perhaps because leadership is gendered and believing otherwise is futile. The best decisions come from a process that benefits from the way different genders communicate and problem solve—just as much as any problem benefits from looking at more than one, default solution.

We have been defining leadership based almost entirely upon how men intuitively approach leading. This really should not be surprising. All elements of the workforce—from the battlefront to the assembly line to the board room—were once the exclusive purview of men. Men defined the standards of professional behavior based on their innate behaviors and understanding of leadership. The characteristics the world assumes to be the attributes of effective leadership are in fact rooted almost entirely in intuitive male behaviors—the adaptation of hunters—not all of which are shared by most women or even all men.

Since the inclusion of women in workforces, the discussion has focused on how women should adapt to prove themselves against these long-held standards. What about changing the standards to reflect a gender diverse workforce? The way a man solves a problem may be brilliant, but it was still not the only solution and is limited to being based on embedded assumptions of the male experience. Women do not need men to explain their thinking to them, men need to respect that there are other ways to think. If we start on a mutual presumption of equality, we can have constructive conversations to solve our world's problems together.

Progress and advancement will come when we

embrace a broader set of innate skills—all of which are relevant in the boardrooms, executive suites, congresses, courthouses, cabinets, and mansions of cities, states, and the federal government. Women have been fighting for equality in a man's world for so long that we do not even realize that our fight has served to validate the assumptive default of human as male. By demanding equality of the overwhelmingly male power-brokers of the world, we enable them to presume it is something they must give us. Equality is ours by nature to wield. We do not need to ask for it.

Men must learn to respect what women already have. This is where empathy becomes such a critical tool. To ratchet back the kicking and screaming, we need to at least try to understand what it is like to be each other, to live a day-in-the-life as the other sex.

VOICES OF AMERICAN WOMEN

#13

Essay by Margarita "Maggie" Angel

The direct answer to how I got into national security was through a random Google search one day in high school. But looking back, I like to think that this was all years in the making. Growing up in a small Chicago suburb, I somehow became interested in a variety of things that I thought were random such as: geography, history, politics, and world languages. In November 2000, I was six years old and I remember asking my dad to explain why states were colored red and blue on the TV screen;

he then explained to me what elections were. At seven years old, I remember vividly the one day in September 2001 that I was not allowed to watch the nightly news with my parents, and later learning the value of patriotism. At eight years old, my mom bought me two study placemats, one with multiplication tables and one with US presidents. To avoid doing math, I memorized presidential facts instead. When I was nine, my favorite telenovela was set in Morocco, so I tried to teach myself Arabic (unfortunately I lost all my progress as an adult).

When I got to high school I continued to excel in history and my French classes, but no one suggested that I continue to pursue these talents in college or as a career. Even my high school guidance counselor never suggested that I pursue a career in international relations or national security, despite my academic success.

So one day when I was a senior in high school, I was trying to figure out where to go to college and what to do with the rest of my life. Naturally, I googled "what careers can I have with a French degree?" since that was the only class I really liked in school. One option was being a translator at the United Nations. I thought that would be cool, so I read more into it and a suggested field of study was international relations. I had never heard of it or knew what it was about, but I applied to colleges that offered it anyway.

My parents and family did not know anything about this field. The people I saw on TV on the news did not look like me, so how was I supposed to know that this was a career path for me? As the only daughter of immigrant parents, I was expected to pick a nice steady "woman's" job, such as an accountant, or a nurse, even though I was scared of needles. Telling them that they were going to pay for a degree that was in the political science department was not well received or understood. But they supported me anyway, probably hoping that I would switch majors and become a nurse or a business major.

When I stepped into my first international relations class on Latin American Politics, everything that I loved came together and it just felt right. I would tell friends and family what I was learning in school, and I would just get awkward smiles and nods since they still had no idea what I was going to do with this degree. At that point, I didn't really know exactly what I was going to do with it, either. However, my professor in undergrad saw my potential and became my mentor in navigating the field of international relations that was completely unfamiliar to me. He helped me apply for internships and research assistantships throughout my college career. He pushed me to do my best, and I will be forever thankful.

At 20 years old, I was accepted into my first internship helping the foreign policy and national security team for my home state Senator. My semester in Washington, DC, changed my life. It was the first time I could see myself working in national security. With every site visit, from the Pentagon to the White House, I felt the possibilities keep opening up and my dreams getting bigger. After a successful internship, my family and friends finally started to understand the field, and I finally started to understand myself. I understood my talents, my passion, and my call to serve my country. As a Latina, I feel a greater responsibility to be in the same room as the most powerful people in the world to give women of color like me a voice.

After that semester, I went on to graduate summa cum laude with a bachelor's in international relations and was accepted to Georgetown University for my master's degree in international security: a true dream come true. I am now in my early career and have enjoyed the challenges that come to approaching contemporary security issues. I'm still not sure if my family and friends know exactly what I do for a living, but now they see me growing in my career, being present in spaces that none of us could have ever imagined.

Technically my career in national security officially started with a Google search, since I had no other connection or insight to this field. But I hope one day in the not-so-distant future, a little girl can watch TV and see someone like her at the Capitol, Pentagon, State Department, and the White House—so she can imagine herself as a policymaker right at that moment and not through a random Google search.

VOICES OF AMERICAN WOMEN

#14

Essay on National Security and Public Health by Sarah Gwinn, UCONN MPH student

Public health policy needs to play a more significant role in our national defense strategy. As a military officer and public health student, I've learned there are many unutilized avenues of public health science that can be used to counter the threats published in the 2018 National Defense Strategy.

The 2018 National Defense Strategy emphasizes inter-state strategic competition, not terrorism, as the primary concern of national security. America's role as a leader of the free world has weakened due to a decreased focus on conflict prevention and human rights. This view has created an opening for Russia and China, near-peer adversaries, to have an insidious influence around the world. Global public health policy, as an arm of our defense strategy, plays a vital role in impeding this influence by promoting social justice, education, job security and gender equality. Destabilization in areas of conflict is exacerbated by health determinants such as poverty, crime, migration, and violence, creating building blocks for gang violence, terrorist groups, and radical organizations. By applying knowledge about health determinants, public health has the ability to decrease violence, mitigate poverty, and decrease migration. This will have a dramatic influence in stabilizing regions and steering governments into a more democratic society.

Public health funding is declining worldwide, and there is an increased need to support health initiatives due to climate change, natural disasters, pandemics, infectious diseases, and cyber threats. In the last 20 years, global pandemics, infectious disease, and climate change have emerged as significant threats to national security. Vulnerable populations have seen catastrophic consequences due to unstable health systems and lack of government support. Our ability to protect our national security interests is interdependent on military and public health measures in these unstable regions. Increased volatile global environments pose short-term and long-term threats that will require international cooperation to address. Tensions over climate change, infectious diseases, and migration will be harder to manage and will lead to conflict and mistrust.

It is imperative we utilize public health's perspective of health determinants to influence the United States' national defense strategy around the world. Safeguarding our standing worldwide will mitigate conflicts, improve health outcomes, and reduce human suffering. Building a stable region requires inclusiveness of its people, government, and military cooperation to provide safety and security among its people. Maintaining a strong public health infrastructure is necessary to building networks of stakeholders that will improve coordination of surveillance and detection systems.

We must understand that the American dream is not everyone's dream, and political structures affect every aspect of society to include health and security. Many governments are inherently fragile due to a predominance of power over institutional norms and political freedoms. They have a vested interest in preventing human development, health, and education. In order for the United States to increase our influence, we must invest in prevention and preparedness, and empower people to make sustained efforts to protect their personal health. Improving health determinates stabilizes populations by reducing inequality, strengthens national governments, impedes near-peer influence, and will protect US national security interests.

Chapter 9

America Should Fight Like a Girl

When the authors of the Declaration of Independence invited the world to judge its cause, they extended that invitation for perpetuity. The founders wanted America's demand for freedom to be observed and scrutinized because they believed in it. They were not afraid of their idea of America being challenged. No good idea suffers from being challenged.

Like our founders, if you believe you have the "right" answer or the "right" way to govern society, you should invite scrutiny and be immune to criticism. If your idea is truly "right," it will survive detractors. Those who force others to believe their beliefs or who bully people who question them demonstrate the fragility of their arguments by fearing scrutiny and challenge. If you have confidence in your ideas and your beliefs, then those who disagree really do not matter. It's still up to you what you choose to believe.

More than just embracing challenge, our Founding Fathers wanted to influence the world and light the torch of self-governance for others to follow. The power of influence is enduring. When you truly influence someone, they take ownership of your idea. When someone takes ownership of your idea, it grows. For competitive people who are always on the defensive, that may be extremely hard. But if you want your ideas and influence to endure, the surest method is to give them away. Isn't that precisely what we do when we raise our children?

As women, "the gatherers," adapted over time to their work of raising children, they learned how to build and wield the power of influence. This is the power that women equate with security more than physical might. Women understand that influence can take an ornery and obstinate child and turn him into an affectionate and cooperative adult. Women know that influence can turn a scared and shy child into a courageous and engaging adult. Women believe that influence can inspire an apathetic child to embrace life and love with abandon.

Those of us who believe in the positive side of humanity, that people can rise above their differences, set aside their hatred and be mutually respectful, that people can embrace diversity and show that love is stronger than hate have been called naive, idealistic, or utopian by the security patriarchy. Even worse, we are often thought of as dangerous because our call for building peace might distract from the process of preparing for war.

But if we toss happiness aside and preserve only the tangibles of our country—the borders, the buildings and bridges, the airways and waterways—what do we have that's worth defending from our enemies? If America were besieged by North Korea, Russia, or even ISIS, why would we even care if we are already living without happiness, love, and warmth? Without hope in the ability to make the next day better than the previous one, what is the point? If we have lost our America and are living in a country with no happiness, joy, kindness, and warmth, what difference does it make who or what is leading the government?

What is more important to secure than love, happiness, and peace?

Furthermore, there is nothing soft or weak about believing in love, happiness, and peace. Believing in peace requires more courage and strength than preparing for war. Believing in peace requires the courage to be hurt, even if most of the time the only damage done is to our pride. For girls who grow up with the expectation that their physical security will be threatened, there is nothing more important to secure than their peace of mind and heart. There is nothing more important than securing who they are.

Girls and women safeguard their authenticity: what they think, believe, and feel. Defiantly preserving the essence of who we are despite fear, violence, and pain is not soft, weak, or defeatist; it is the very definition of strength.

This is where our nation could learn a lot from something the #MeToo Movement has made painfully clear. Demonstrating resistance to being manipulated and showing determination to speak your truth is creating your own security born of surviving a world without the guarantee of safety. This is how half of America's population experiences security. This is girl security.

Right now, in this moment, America needs this strength and security. If we are going to endure as a nation of free people in a world inundated with information, narratives, and images that seek to divide us, we must be stronger than we have been. We need the courage of conviction and the will to remain independent despite being attacked, exploited, humiliated, and dehumanized. This world is calling us to demonstrate a greater courage than what is required to survive physical pain. This kind of courage requires us to work together and set aside the potential of wounded pride. Hate currently divides us. Resentment and spite dissolve the bonds that civility creates. While it is infinitely easier to be angry at others for the real woes and grievances of our lives, the logical progression of that hostility is a life of isolation. What can any of us solve alone?

When America has taken the time it needs to reflect upon its good and bad behaviors, and is ready to end its time-out, we need this kind of courage and strength. National resistance to those who tell us what to think, what to say, how to vote, who we should like, and who we should hate, is what will keep us independent. National courage to tolerate what we oppose is what will keep us *united*.

VOICES OF AMERICAN WOMEN

#15

Essay by Rachel Jones, B.A. in Religious Studies,
University of Virginia

When I express that I am interested in peace and reconciliation research, people often pause and offer a sympathetic look that denotes their feeling that peace is nonexistent within the reality of violence and terror in the world. I understand this response or inclination to believe that peace is something that is unachievable and idealistic, but believing peace is possible is one of the most courageous acts. Peace and reconciliation requires much of ourselves, assessing our own vulnerabilities in conversation with others' "otherness."

Contrary to what some believe, peace and security are not in opposition. Actually, I believe that working towards peace allows us to work towards personal, national, and collective security.

As a millennial, I am very familiar with the need for security and the lack of security we have. I grew up around the consistent rhetoric of terrorism, as I was in kindergarten when the horrors of 9/11 occurred, and I do not remember life prior to terrorism. News and culture reflected the looming fear of national security and it became integrated into my personal understanding of security. Due to the cultural and national fear of others and their extreme desire for strong security, I became scared of others who were similar to those portrayed as threats to our national security. As I grew up, through various encounters with people from other cultures, I realized that my personal security wasn't actually secure when I built up my walls or stood guard around groups of others.

My first year of college, I lived in Philadelphia, PA, which was vastly different from my upper-middle class suburban upbringing. I was thrown into the midst of a bustling and diverse city. At least once a week I encountered homeless persons on my way to class. After a short while, I started regularly volunteering with an organization that served some of the city's unsheltered and unfed. I expected to walk into the space and be ready to give people what they wanted—food. What I encountered, however, was an extremely informed organization that runs its food service in a trauma-informed way, continually emphasizing to their servers and the guests that there are to be no lines and that there will be exactly enough food for everyone—not abundance, but enough.

I volunteered weekly with this organization, enjoying regular conversations with guests and other helpers. Eventually, I realized that their trauma-informed method shaped my understanding of my own relationship to the others present. It became clear that their "we will have enough" policy showed me that oftentimes in my life and in our society, we combat scarcity with abundance or we don't address the scarcity of resources at all. This space offered another viewpoint: there is enough. As a guest, this means that you are not a competitor with other people walking in wanting to be seated and served. Not only does the idea of "enough" help to combat competitiveness and frustration regarding receiving the practical resources of food, it also shifts our mindsets to see those at our table, those we walk by on the street, and those we encounter in our lives, as people or neighbors instead of competitors for resources.

Through time in distinct cultures across the globe, I have seen how scarcity of resources can create or spark extreme violence and hate. I have seen that tipping the scales between abundance and the threat of scarcity can drive corruption, secrecy, scheming, and greed. Peace and security will only come when we stop viewing resources as limited and in turn stop seeing our neighbors or neighboring countries as competitors we must defeat in the race for these resources. Peace and security come when we recognize that we, too, are vulnerable and susceptible to scarcity, but we choose to recognize that our vulnerabilities are not equivalent to weaknesses and that our neighbors are also vulnerable in the face of scarcity.

There is bravery required when we work towards peace. Peace requires us to look; to stop what we are doing and really learn what is happening in others' experiences. In our looking, we can admit that we don't know everything, that there is more to know and others might be able to offer that knowledge. In admitting our limits, we can accept ourselves and others, as is, instead of feeling that we need to have everything. In accepting that there are limits on what we need, we can open ourselves up to sharing our resources with the knowledge that we all still can thrive. While we commune together, while we share resources and learn about each other, our minds and our perspectives change in big and small ways. Ultimately, our idea of peace and security shifts, involving not just the concepts that are familiar, but also those that are new and emerging.

Let's believe peace is possible. Let's believe that peace is not at odds with security. And let's work continually towards coming together, to prioritize the collective security that protects both security and peace, at both national and personal levels.

VOICES OF AMERICAN WOMEN

#16

Girl Security essay by Avery

I can remember distinctly the day of the Boston Marathon bombing. I was on April vacation in 5th grade, sitting in a restaurant booth in Pembroke, Massachusetts. My mom turned towards the TV positioned above the bar, and I heard her say, "Oh my God, the Boston

Marathon was bombed." I wasn't exactly sure what that meant, but my mom was scared. We stayed at home for the rest of the break, skipping our trip to the Boston Aquarium. When I returned to school the next week, my teacher sat us down for a discussion. I thought she would explain to us what had happened, but instead she told us that she wasn't allowed to discuss it. She said we could go to the guidance counselor if we felt scared. I remember raising my hand to ask, "Why aren't we allowed to talk about it?"

I think a defining difference between my generation and my teacher's is that she once lived in a world where terrorism wasn't a constant threat. My generation wants to talk about these things even though they scare us. We want to solve these problems so that perhaps the next generation will not feel the same fear, yet we have grown accustomed to hearing, "You're too young to understand."

I was born within the first months of the post-9/11 world in May 2002. My understanding of national security was determined by the timing of my entrance into a world that was experiencing a newfound fear of extremism. The post-9/11 generation has known terrorism, long-standing war, and the looming threat of nuclear conflict since the day we were born. While we have grown into the roles of advocates and change-makers, we are becoming numb to news about school shootings, terrorist attacks, and other global crises. My mother's initial reaction to the Boston bombings was that of disbelief, while I was simply reminded of the chronic fear that plagues my generation.

People my age are beginning to understand that the system set before us is not one that will serve us if not reformed. To us, national security is a feeling. It's what comes of the fear that rests at the back of my mind, lying dormant until I hear word of another attack. Above all, national security is a conversation, one that we need to have with young people who have never seen a world without violence and war. My generation cannot change the future of the world if we as a nation are too scared to discuss these issues we face.

Step 5:

Praise the Next Good Thing America Does

Once you have ended your child's time-out, it is critical to lavish praise on the next few good things your child does. Because children are always in learning mode, positive reinforcement is a critical motivator and shaper of future behavior. It may feel like a stretch for the parent, but that little extra few seconds of praise matters more than a long, drawn-out scolding later on. It doesn't really matter what the good behavior is, big or small, easy or hard; what matters is that you acknowledge it with a smile, a hug, or verbal praise. This is equally true when America and Americans do something good. Traditional media has rarely covered good news as part of its service to the country. But social media makes it much easier to share and amplify the acts of kindness, courage, compassion, and love that we see every day. Taking a few seconds to acknowledge it with a thumbs up, reposting, or retweet, is more powerful than obsessing about the latest complaint, scandal, or conspiracy theory.

As I close this narrative, I wonder what good deed will America do. What kindness will Americans show each other? Will it only come in the aftermath of a devastating national tragedy, another mass shooting, a political storm, or a real weather crisis? Will we remember that America is entrusted to each of us? As individuals we make America whatever it is.

I look forward to watching what the Millennial and Z Generations do. All five of my children fall into these two generations and most of my students as well. I have so much faith in them. They are collaborative. They understand the importance of goodness in life and courageously question the hyper-competitive and obsessive workaholics of the Baby Boomers and their offspring, Generation X. They care about nature and nurture and being connected.

My children and I, along with their dad, run the range of political and ideological beliefs. We do not agree on the Second Amendment, for example. My second son is a staunch supporter of gun ownership rights. His youngest siblings, who walked out of school during the protests organized in support of the Marjory Stoneman Douglas High School shooting victims, do not agree. Their father hunts, and I have been trained in the use of multiple weapons, and have been in places where I was grateful for that.

Ultimately, while we disagree among the seven of us very passionately, we do so with respect for the feelings of each other. None of us believes that a Constitutionally given right, of any kind, should be taken away even for public safety. Just as none of us believes Americans, from politicians to lobbyists to the Chairman of the Joint Chiefs of Staff of our Armed Forces has fully and objectively considered the many options that could reduce the Second Amendment controversy. We are Americans. We should be able to protect the right granted in the Second Amendment to all Americans to own a weapon while also reducing that weapon's enablement of those who intend to take away our most fundamental right to life. If we only had our Founding Fathers and Mothers to say to us, "Lower your voice and let's talk calmly and respect-fully about how we can solve this. You both deserve to be heard."

I have learned in the past ten years how to truly live life to its fullest, with love, peace, joy, meaning, and security from my children, my students, and my many Millennial colleagues. I wish they could take the lead in America, from sea to shining sea, right now!

I welcome hearing of America's good deeds and will be happy to join in praising her for the effort and courage it takes to try. Imagine drowning out the hate speech, the name-calling, and the finger-pointing with civility. I remember a pastor who once pondered how so many of his congregation members could leave a house of God only to be discourteous and hostile to each other when they got in their cars to exit the parking lot. It seems a civil tongue is the first thing to go, and thus the most important virtue to demonstrate.

As I mentioned earlier, I believe that good ideas should be given away, not hoarded. I have faith that Americans with the courage to hope will find endless ways to do good every day. Should you seek inspiration, though, Girl Security is ready to offer it. This nonpartisan, nonprofit organization was founded by Lauren Bean Buitta to empower girls with the understanding of national security early enough in their formative stages to inspire their participation in it as leaders of the future. Lauren had the courage to create a solution to the per-sistent problem of the lack of gender parity in national security leadership by building a mechanism for change. I say courage because Girl Security requires patience. And it requires the fortitude to withstand those who criticize its premise. And as importantly, it requires boys and men to realize that "Man the Hunter's" definition of national security has always only been half of the reality. Men need to know the other half, too. Knowledge will make us smarter. Cooperation will make us stronger.

The rest of this book is not mine to write. It is up to all of you to author America's future.

VOICES OF AMERICAN WOMEN

#17

Words of encouragement from a founding mother to an adolescent America

My Dear America,

Lend me a moment of your time before this chance passes. I can see that you are in a rush, but I do not think you know what you are rushing toward. You are determined, but you do not know what you are determined to do. You are confident, but I fear your limited competence does not merit such self-assuredness. You are strong, but you are squandering your strength on futile endeavors. You are fearless, but you are not using your courage to protect and fight for those who cannot. You are smart and innovative, but you are not putting those talents toward the greater good. You are vibrant and unique, and yet you are too obsessed with being the same as everyone else.

My dear child, please reflect on who you have been and who you can be; just for a moment before it is too late. I have watched you from afar, marveling at your development. When I braved the dark and damp cobblestones and muddy paths of Manhattan in the middle of the night to pass a small fragment of information to a fellow member of General Washington's spy ring, I never imagined that the breakaway government we would forge would include my voice. How excited I was to learn that women were given this extraordinary honor of electing their representatives in the government that General Washington and the Continentals fought to create.

But I have also wept at the many sources of pain you have endured, such as the great world wars and the fear of those weapons of hell you call atomic bombs. I have sobbed even harder, and nearly despaired for your survival, at the bloodshed you inflicted upon yourself during the war between the North and the South. I have feared for you during all the wars—from Korea and Vietnam to Afghanistan and Iraq. I prayed while watching the horrific destruction of your great monuments to progress on September 11. And I shuddered at the thought of the constant fear and hardship you endured during the Great Depression and the Cold War.

There was a time when what you called a "cold war" ended, and I thought you would benefit from the peace dividend and be the world's great glowing light. But it seems without an enemy with which to contrast yourself, you lost your fundamental identity.

My son was too small when he was taken from me. But I imagine that he would have faced some of the same fears that you do now. Had my son lived, he would have come to that time of his life when he would need to choose his own approach. I have wondered often, would he have gone into the unfamiliar territory of the future with a smile on his face, seeking friendship and offering his own? Would he have walked with purpose? Would he have shown fear or masked it by being aggressive?

Or would he have floundered without my hand and heart to guide him?

You are so much like this child, thrashing about and trying a little of every approach. You have been inconsistent and noncommittal. You have changed courses without noticing the repercussions to all who look to you as a leader. A child who behaves like that will make few loyal friends, and even fewer admirers.

America, be as we were during the Revolution: brave, but not brazen. Be humble, though not arrogant; still be confident in your cause of freedom. Be wise, not cynical. Be kind, not self-absorbed. Be bold, not cautious; but do not use boldness to disrespect others or to behave recklessly. Be honest, not duplicitous when you are embarrassed by your mistakes. You can never lie to a watching world. The world will always be looking to you, my dear America. Dare to be the ideal. For if someday the world stops watching, you will slink into the forgotten pages of history. This is not where I wish you to be.

Above all things that you should strive to be, be you. Be the America I fought to birth. Along with so many others who died to establish a new nation, believe in the unalienable rights of all to life, liberty, and the pursuit of happiness. And while you hold to this ideal, "mutually pledge to each other your Lives, your Fortunes, and your sacred Honor," because you are all my children. And each of you is part of one family.

With affection and a heart full of hope,
Your loving mother, 355

As with the rest of history, America's story is mostly known through the narratives of men. While it is impossible to bring to life all the experiences and expertise of the women who were critical to the idea of America, there is one story I would like to surface.

Agent 355 was a female member of George Washington's New York-based spy network known as the Culper Ring. She is a lady of mystery lost to history. Most historians agree she was from a well-respected, wealthy family that was likely loyal to the British Crown during the Revolutionary War. Her access to British officers in intimate settings enabled her to uncover Benedict Arnold's plan to surrender the strategically important West Point to the British Army. West Point was not only a military institute; it also was a major armory for the Continental Army and a critical fort commanding the Hudson River. In the hands of the Crown, West Point might have given the British a strategic advantage to win the war. Agent 355 found out and got the information to General Washington in time to prevent Arnold from taking command of West Point before turning to the British. Americans have not heard of Agent 355, but we have much to thank her for.

While the other members of the Culper Spy Ring have been identified because most revealed their roles during their own lifetimes, Agent 355 remains shrouded in mystery. Historians believe she died in captivity following a British sweeping arrest of friends who socialized in the same circles as Benedict Arnold and the British spymaster who turned him. However she perished, one thing is clear: Agent 355 never gave up her identity or betrayed her fellow spies. She is one of America's best kept secrets, but her heroic story is one that the world should know. She is a lost hero of the American Revolution and the founding mother of the intelligence profession in the United States.

Benjamin Franklin once said, "Three men can keep a secret, if two of them are dead." With all due respect to a Founding Father, clearly Mr. Franklin had never met a female spy.

What is all the more remarkable, and the most powerful lesson to draw from Agent 355's self-sacrifice, is that she did it

all in service for a revolution that fought for liberty and equality,
but not hers. Who among us today would sacrifice our life to
bestow upon others the very thing we desire for ourselves, know-
ing it will still be denied to us?

VOICES OF AMERICAN WOMEN

#18

A letter from the author

To Donald J. Trump,

In 1993, when very few knew who Osama Bin Laden
was or the threat his group would pose, I was a young
terrorism analyst working in the Intelligence Community. It was a confusing time in the early post-Cold War
world. No one wanted to believe a single individual without the massive resources of a nation state could be a
significant terrorist threat to the United States. So to help
explain the tremendous power of influence that one
person could wield, I compared Bin Laden to someone
everyone did know at that time: a public figure who had
a bold vision that many others had dismissed as impossible, but whose charisma and wherewithal were enough
to see that vision come true. I compared Osama Bin
Laden to you.

I did not know in that moment how accurate and
enduring that comparison would be. Like you, Bin Laden
saw his vision through. He derailed America's purpose
in this world—to be a beacon of hope for those who seek
nothing more than the simple freedom to pursue their

life, liberty, and happiness without being targets of hatred, vilification, and violence. He bankrupted America and divided us from each other. In doing so, Bin Laden and his followers revealed to other adversaries the vulnerability of what was once America's greatest strength, the strength we embraced and relied upon to defeat totalitarianism in the Cold War. That strength was our deep-rooted tolerance of diversity, our rejection of tyranny of the majority, our embrace of checks and balances; in other words, our Constitution.

Osama Bin Laden, like all men of evil with their serpent's tongues, persuaded a handful of men to place themselves above the God they worshipped and judge the worth of human beings based on their gender, race, religion, ethnicity, nationality, culture, and core identity. He did all this through the power of influence. Bin Laden did not fly the planes into the World Trade Center, the Pentagon or across the Pennsylvania sky. Bin Laden never shot a weapon into a crowd or detonated a suicide vest. He used his words to motivate others to kill for him.

And so have you.

But just as we have refused to relent to our foreign adversaries' influence on America, so too will we refuse to listen to your calls for more hate, more violence, and more divisiveness.

Gina M. Bennett

ACKNOWLEDGEMENTS

Everything I do takes a village. I am so fortunate to live in an extraordinarily supportive village. I'd like to thank a few of them for their kindness, expertise, and time in helping me with this project, starting with Nancy Cleary for still having faith in me after ten long years of wondering what she got herself into.

To my team of wonderful misfits at work in DSOP, and especially my fellow NABsters, thank you for caring so much about so many people who will never know to thank you. Your service and inexhaustible friendship is a source of inspiration to me. And to Matt, for reading and almost being honest about everything I wrote (yeah, I know you sugarcoated).

To my fabulous students at Georgetown—you give me so much hope! Thank you for trusting me and sharing your wisdom with me and each other. Keep geeking out on ethics. You are the leaders who deserve to lead.

I will never be able to put into words how much meaning Jody Williams has given my life, but I will keep trying to express it. To her, and all the wonderful women and men of the Alturas Institute, thank you for going out on the ledge with me. Over and over and over (hint: I'm not done).

To Lauren, the brilliant founder of Girl Security, I wish we had met when we were little girls. Just think of how we could have changed the world! Oh wait, we are!

To my sister and her wonderful family and to my co-parent extraordinaire, and to Bert, thanks for believing in me and for always having my back.

Collette, I owe you so much for sharing the love of your life with me. Without Ken and his huge heart and big Texan hug, I would never have believed in the beauty inside of me. You are both such special people, and I wish all the dark corners of the world could experience the joy, love, and generosity you always share with me.

To Colleen, whose life has so strangely paralleled mine (or is it the other way around?), thank you for being the best friend a person could ask for through some of the hardest of times. I do hope my life is following yours!

Thank you, Jeannine, for knowing when it hurt and when I needed to feel it.

Araj—"We should buy a bar!"

JB, thanks for being my bodyguard and beast of burden, my dance partner, and so much more.

To all the girls and women whose frustrations, visions for the future, and aspirations for all women are captured in these few pages, I cannot thank you enough. Your trust and courage inspire so many, including myself, every minute of every day.

(continued list of signatories from p.54) An Open Letter to the National Security Community

Affiliations are for identification purposes only and do not represent organizational views or positions of the U.S. Government

* Indicates former affiliation or title, as appropriate

Mrs. Ana Janaina Nelson, Southern Cone Regional Security Officer, U.S. Department of State*

Ambassador (ret.) Wanda L. Nesbitt

Ambassador (ret.) Crystal Nix-Hines

Ms. Suzanne Nossel, Executive Director, PEN America

Ms. Nneoma Veronica Nwog, Adjunct Professor of Law, Washington College of Law, American University

Dr. Olga Oliker, Center for Strategic and International Studies

Ms. Kimberly Olson, U.S. Department of State*

Ambassador (ret.) Adrienne S. O'Neal

Ms. Won Palisoul, Founder, Women Veterans and Families Network (WVFN)

Ms. Michelle Parker, Foreign Service Officer, U.S. Agency for International Development

Ms. Susan Parker-Burns, Foreign Service Officer, U.S. Department of State

Ms. Mira Patel, Secretary's Policy Planning Staff, U.S. Department of State*

Ambassador (ret.) Cynthia Shepard Perry

Ms. Heather Peterson, RAND Corporation*

Ms. Shainell Pruitt

Ms. Vera Ranola, Council on Foreign Relations

Dr. Mira Rapp-Hooper, Yale Law School

Ambassador Eunice Reddick

Ms. Alissa Redmond, Foreign Service Officer,U.S. Department of State

Ms. Susan Reichle, Career Minister, U.S. Agency for International Development*

Ms. Emily Renard, U.S. Departments of Defense and State*

Ms. Brenan Richards, Department of Defense

Ms. Rachel Rizzo, Center for a New American Security

Ms. Erin S. Robertson, U.S. Department of State

Colonel (retired) Kabrena Rodda, U.S. Air Force

Ms. Lisa Roman, U.S. Department of State*

Ambassador (ret.) Doria Rosen

Ms. Laura Rosenberger, U.S. Department of State* and National Security Council*

Ms. Carey Rudell, Foreign Service Officer, U.S. Department of State*

Ambassador (ret.) Robin Sanders

Ambassador (ret.) Janet A. Sanderson

Ambassador (ret.) Teresita Schaffer

Ambassador (ret.) Brenda Brown Schoonover

Dr. Tammy S. Schultz, Marine Corps War College

Ms. Sarah Sewall, Under Secretary of State*

Captain Margaret Seymour, U.S. Marine Corps Reserves

Mrs. Rina Shah, Founder, The Prigova Group

Ambassador (ret.) Dana Shell Smith

Ms. Lindsey Sheppard Draper

Ms. Jolynn Shoemaker, Executive Director, Women In International Security (WIIS)*

Ms. Joan Sinclair, Foreign Service Officer, U.S. Department of State

Dr. Amanda Sloat, U.S. Department of State*

Ms. Julie Smith, Deputy National Security Advisor to the Vice President*

Ms. Lachlyn Soper, Foreign Service Officer, U.S. Department of State

Ms. Rachel Sorey, Foreign Service Officer, U.S. Agency for International Development

Ms. Erin Soto, Senior Foreign Service, U.S. Agency for International Development*

Ms. Monica Stein-Olson, Career Minister, U.S. Agency for International Development

Ms. Mary Stickles, Foreign Service Officer, U.S. Department of State

Ambassador (ret.) Cynthia Stroum

Ms. Kelsey Suemnicht, Founder, The Foreign Policy Project

Ms. Caroline Tess, Special Assistant to the President*

Ambassador (ret.) Linda Thomas-Greenfield

Ms. Christine Trostle

Ms. Paula Uribe, Senior Advisor to the Assistant Secretary of State for Western Hemisphere Affairs, U.S. Department of State*

Ms. Toni Verstandig, Deputy Assistant Secretary of State Bureau of Near Eastern Affairs, U.S. Department of State*

Ambassador (ret.) Marcelle M. Wahba, The Arab Gulf States Institute in Washington

Dr. Nancy J. Walker, Director, Africa Center for Strategic Studies, Department of Defense*

Ms. Roslyn Warren, Georgetown Institute for Women, Peace and Security*

Ms. Lynne Weil, U.S. Department of State* and Broadcasting Board of Governors*

Dr. Sharon White, Senior Foreign Service Officer, U.S. Department of State*

Ambassador (ret.) Bisa Williams

Dr. Tamara Wittes, The Brookings Institution

Dr. Jaime Yassif, Department of Defense*

Dr. Sarah Yerkes, U.S. Department of State*

Ms. Vera Zakem

Ms. Michelle Ziegler, Analyst, Department of Defense and Department of Homeland Security

ENDNOTES

[1] **Girl Security** is a nonprofit, nonpartisan educational organization designed by women to engage girls in the mission and careers of national security. https://www.girlsecurity.org/

[2] https://www.cdc.gov/parents/essentials/timeout/steps.html

[3] *Idea of America: Reflections on the Birth of the United States* by Gordon Wood, Chapter 2.

[4] Bennett, Gina. "Cultural Relativism in Foreign Policy." Lecture, Ethics in Intelligence and National Security Decisions from Georgetown University, Washington, DC, January 22, 2019.

[5] *How Good People Make Tough Choices*, Rushworth Kidder, 109.

[6] (Kidder, 139).

[7] (Kidder, 124).

[8] *Idea of America: Reflections on the Birth of the United States*, Gordon Wood.

[9] Bennett, Gina. "Ethics in Intelligence Support to Policy." Lecture, Ethics in Intelligence and National Security Decisions from Georgetown University, Washington, DC, February 8, 2019.

[10] (Kidder, 127).

[11] https://www.stimson.org/sites/default/files/file-attachments/CT_Spending_Report_0.pdf

[12] https://www.nsc.org/work-safety/tools-resources/injury-facts/chart

[13] These numbers come from the Georgetown Institute for Women, Peace and Security, the UN, and US Child Protective Services, among other resources. https://giwps.georgetown.edu/the-index/

[14] https://www.theatlantic.com/national/archive/2013/01/america-has-an-incest-problem/272459/

[15] https://www.rainn.org/statistics/children-and-teens;
i. Department of Justice, Office of Justice Programs, Bureau of Justice Statistics, National Crime Victimization Survey, 2010-2016 (2017);
ii. Federal Bureau of Investigation, National Incident-Based Reporting System, 2012-2016 (2017);

iii. Federal Bureau of Investigation, National Incident-Based Reporting System, 2012-2016 (2017);

iv. Department of Justice, Office of Justice Programs, Bureau of Justice Statistics, Felony Defendants in Large Urban Counties, 2009 (2013).

(This statistic combines information from several federal government reports. Because it combines data from studies with different methodologies, it is an approximation, not a scientific estimate. Please see the original sources for more detailed information. These statistics are updated annually and as new information is published.)

[16] United States Department of Health and Human Services, Administration for Children and Families, Administration on Children, Youth and Families, Children's Bureau. Child Mal-treatment Survey, 2016 (2018).

1. Department of Justice, Office of Justice Programs, Bureau of Justice Statistics, Sex Offenses and Offenders (1997).

2. David Finkelhor, Anne Shattuck, Heather A. Turner, & Sherry L. Hamby, The Lifetime Prevalence of Child Sexual Abuse and Sexual Assault Assessed in Late Adolescence, 55 Journal of Adolescent Health 329, 329-333 (2014).

3. Department of Justice, Office of Justice Programs, Bureau of Justice Statistics, Sexual Assault of Young Children as Reported to Law Enforcement (2000).

[17] Department of Justice, Office of Justice Programs, Bureau of Justice Statistics, Female Victims of Sexual Violence, 1994-2010 (2013).

[18] https://datausa.io/profile/soc/333050/

[19] https://www.pewresearch.org/fact-tank/2018/10/09/how-the-world-views-the-u-s-and-its-president-in-9-charts/

[20] https://www.annenbergpublicpolicycenter.org/americans-are-poorly-informed-about-basic-constitutional-provisions/

Take Action

Follow @GirlSecurity